Multiplication of Larger Numbers

> Turn to each section to find a more detailed skills list.

Y0-CDJ-802

Table of Contents

What Does This Book Include?

- More than 80 student practice pages that build basic math skills
- A detailed skills list for each section of the book
- Send-home letters informing parents of the skills being targeted and ways to practice these skills
- Student checkups
- A reproducible student progress chart
- Reproducible grids to use with students who need help aligning numbers properly when writing vertical multiplication problems
- Awards to celebrate student progress
- Answer keys for easy checking
- Perforated pages for easy removal and filing if desired

What Are the Benefits of This Book?

- Organized for quick and easy use
- Enhances and supports your existing math program
- Offers four reproducible practice pages for each multiplication skill
- Provides reinforcement for different ability levels
- Includes communication pages that encourage parents' participation in their children's learning of math
- Contains checkups that assess students' multiplication knowledge
- Offers a reproducible chart for documenting student progress
- Aligns with national math standards

Manufactured in the United States
10 9 8 7 6 5 4 3 2

How to Use This Book
Steps to Success

Choose Skills to Target

Scan the detailed table of contents at the beginning of each section to find just the right skills to target your students' needs.

Select Fun Practice Pages

Choose from a variety of fun formats the pages that best match your students' current ability levels.

Fun Formats

Date Skill Completed

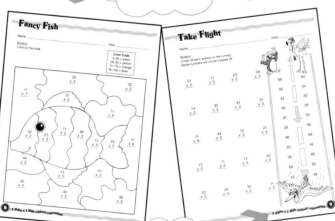

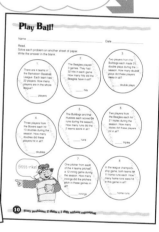

Targeted Skill

Letter to Parents Informing Them of Skill to Review

Communicate With Parents

Recruit parent assistance by locating the appropriate parent letter (pages 104–118), making copies, and sending the letter home.

Problems for Practice

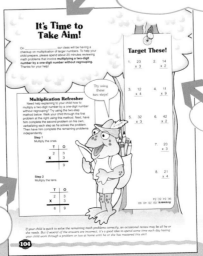

Multiplication Review for Parents

Assess Student Understanding

Assess students' progress with student checkups (mini tests) on pages 105–119. Choose Checkup A or Checkup B.

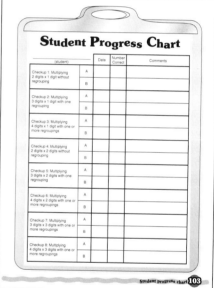

Checkup 1

Name _____ Date _____

A. 32 x 3	11 x 8	12 x 2	21 x 4	22 x 3
B. 14 x 2	42 x 2	12 x 3	20 x 4	11 x 5
C. 44 x 2	33 x 3	21 x 2	34 x 2	11 x 3
D. 11 x 7	30 x 2	20 x 3	24 x 2	23 x 3

Test A: 2 digits x 1 digit without regrouping

Checkup 1

Name _____ Date _____

A. 23 x 2	30 x 3	33 x 2	43 x 2	22 x 4
B. 11 x 6	12 x 4	31 x 3	40 x 2	22 x 2
C. 30 x 3	32 x 2	11 x 9	41 x 2	21 x 3
D. 13 x 2	31 x 2	13 x 3	14 x 2	11 x 4

Test B: 2 digits x 1 digit without regrouping

Two Checkups for Each Skill

Document Progress

Documenting student progress can be as easy as 1, 2, 3! Do the following for each student:

1. Make a copy of the student progress chart (page 103).
2. File the chart in his math portfolio or a class notebook.
3. Record the date each checkup is given, the number of correct answers, and any comments regarding his progress.

Student Progress Chart

_____ (student)

		Date	Number Correct	Comments
Checkup 1: Multiplying 2 digits x 1 digit without regrouping	A			
	B			
Checkup 2: Multiplying 3 digits x 1 digit with one regrouping	A			
	B			
Checkup 3: Multiplying 4 digits x 1 digit with one or more regroupings	A			
	B			
Checkup 4: Multiplying 2 digits x 2 digits without regrouping	A			
	B			
Checkup 5: Multiplying 3 digits x 2 digits with one regrouping	A			
	B			
Checkup 6: Multiplying 4 digits x 2 digits with one or more regroupings	A			
	B			
Checkup 7: Multiplying 3 digits x 3 digits with one or more regroupings	A			
	B			
Checkup 8: Multiplying 4 digits x 3 digits with one or more regroupings	A			
	B			

Student progress chart 103

Celebrate!

Celebrate multiplication success using the awards on pages 122–124.

Congratulations!

_____ knows how to multiply by **1 digit!**

Multiplying by 1 Digit Award

Teacher _____

Date _____

You hit the multiplication target!

122

Books in the Target Math Success series include

- *Basic Addition Facts to 18*
- *Basic Subtraction Facts to 18*
- *Addition of Larger Numbers*
- *Subtraction of Larger Numbers*
- *Basic Multiplication Facts and More*
- *Basic Division Facts and More*
- *Multiplication of Larger Numbers*
- *Division of Larger Numbers*
- *Fractions*
- *Decimals*

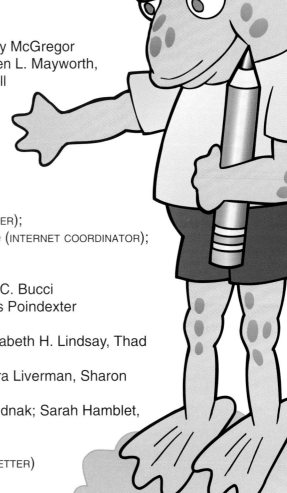

Managing Editor: Peggy W. Hambright
Editor at Large: Diane Badden
Staff Editors: Lauren E. Cox, Debra Liverman, Sherry McGregor
Copy Editors: Tazmen Carlisle, Amy Kirtley-Hill, Karen L. Mayworth, Kristy Parton, Debbie Shoffner, Cathy Edwards Simrell
Cover Artist: Kimberly Richard
Art Coordinator: Pam Crane
Artists: Pam Crane, Theresa Lewis Goode, Clevell Harris, Ivy L. Koonce, Clint Moore, Greg D. Rieves, Rebecca Saunders, Barry Slate, Stuart Smith, Donna K. Teal
Contributing Artist: Cathy Spangler Bruce
The Mailbox® Books.com: Judy P. Wyndham (MANAGER); Jennifer Tipton Bennett (DESIGNER/ARTIST); Karen White (INTERNET COORDINATOR); Paul Fleetwood, Xiaoyun Wu (SYSTEMS)

President, The Mailbox Book Company™: Joseph C. Bucci
Director of Book Planning and Development: Chris Poindexter
Curriculum Director: Karen P. Shelton
Book Development Managers: Cayce Guiliano, Elizabeth H. Lindsay, Thad McLaurin
Editorial Planning: Kimberley Bruck (DIRECTOR); Debra Liverman, Sharon Murphy, Susan Walker (TEAM LEADERS)
Editorial and Freelance Management: Karen A. Brudnak; Sarah Hamblet, Hope Rodgers (EDITORIAL ASSISTANTS)
Editorial Production: Lisa K. Pitts (TRAFFIC MANAGER); Lynette Dickerson (TYPE SYSTEMS); Mark Rainey (TYPESETTER)
Librarian: Dorothy C. McKinney

www.themailbox.com

Multiplication of Larger Numbers

Multiplication of Larger Numbers

Table of Contents

Parent Communication and Student Checkups

*See pages 104–119 for corresponding parent communications and student checkups (mini tests) for these skills.

Path to the Party

Name _____ Date _____

Multiply.
Color the boxes with answers greater than 50 to show the path.

Start

32 x 3	42 x 2	20 x 4	30 x 3
13 x 2	12 x 4	22 x 2	11 x 3	31 x 3
43 x 2	33 x 2	21 x 4	23 x 3	22 x 4
11 x 9	12 x 3	12 x 2	14 x 2	13 x 3
32 x 2	40 x 2			

Finish

2 digits x 1 digit without regrouping

Fancy Fish

Name _____ Date _____

Multiply.
Color by the code.

Color Code
0–25 = green
26–50 = yellow
51–75 = orange
76–100 = blue

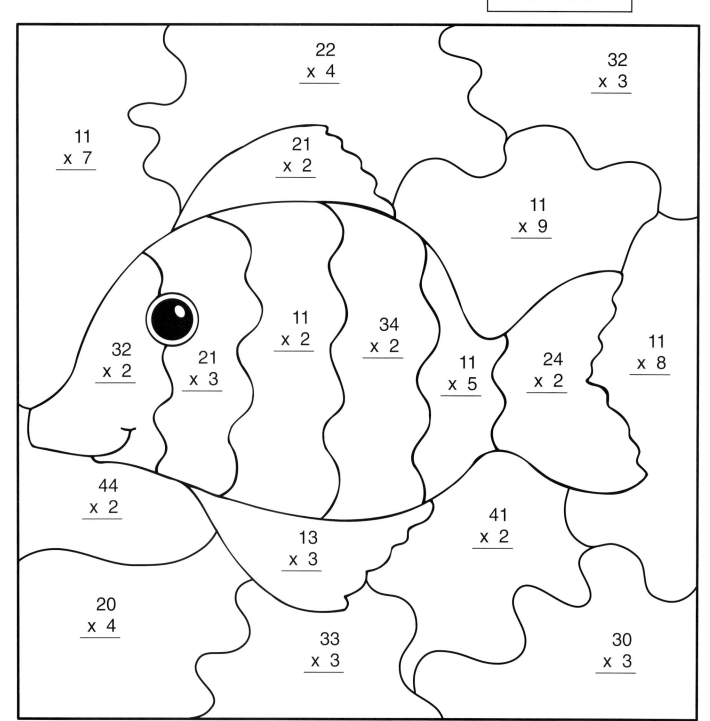

2 digits x 1 digit without regrouping

Take Flight

Multiply.
Cross off each answer on the runway.
Some numbers will not be crossed off.

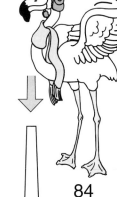

21 x 2	11 x 5	23 x 3	24 x 2
14 x 2	30 x 3	41 x 2	31 x 3
11 x 6	43 x 2	12 x 2	21 x 4
13 x 2	11 x 4	12 x 3	40 x 2
23 x 2	22 x 4	30 x 2	11 x 3

66   84
82   24
44   32
60   26
80   55
28   86
46   69
93   42
36   88
68   90
33   48

Play Ball!

Name _____ Date _____

Read.
Solve each problem on another sheet of paper.
Write the answer in the blank.

1.

There are 4 teams in the Barkstown Baseball League. Each team has 22 players. How many players are in the whole league?

_____ players

2.

The Beagles played 3 games. They had 32 hits in each game. How many hits did the Beagles have in all?

_____ hits

3.

Two players from the Bulldogs each made 31 double plays during the season. How many double plays did these players make in all?

_____ double plays

4.

Three players from the Boxers each hit 13 doubles during the season. How many doubles did these players hit in all?

_____ doubles

5.

The Bulldogs and the Huskies each scored 34 runs during the season. How many runs did the 2 teams score in all?

_____ runs

6.

Two players from the Beagles each hit 21 triples during the season. How many triples did these players hit in all?

_____ triples

Sttt-rike!

7.

One pitcher from each of the 4 teams pitched a 12-inning game during the season. How many innings did the pitchers pitch in these games in all?

_____ innings

8.

In the league championship game, both teams hit 11 home runs each. How many home runs were hit in this game in all?

_____ home runs

©The Education Center, Inc. • *Target Math Success* • TEC60831 • Key p. 126

Story problems: 2 digits x 1 digit without regrouping

Mail Me!

Name _____   Date _____

Multiply.
Show your work.
To show the path to the mailbox, color the
  envelopes whose answers are less than 450.

Hurry! The mailman
is on his way!

Start

213 x 2	123 x 2	321 x 2

301 x 2	133 x 3	231 x 3	233 x 3

123 x 3	234 x 2	321 x 3	203 x 3

211 x 2	132 x 3

312 x 3	332 x 3

Gotta Have a Gumball!

Multiply.
Show your work.
Color by the code.

Between 0 and 300	Between 301 and 600	Between 601 and 1,000
Pink	Yellow	Blue

311
x   3

110
x   3

312
x   2

131
x   3

121
x   2

210
x   3

214
x   2

411
x   2

444
x   2

101
x   2

895
x   1

343
x   2

111
x   2

222
x   2

432
x   2

114
x   2

404
x   2

244
x   2

440
x   2

120
x   3

Clarabell's Crossing

Name _____ Date _____

Multiply.
Show your work.
To solve the riddle, match the letters to the numbered lines below.

I made it across!

231 x 2 = G	320 x 3 = T

210 x 3 = O	518 x 1 = H	441 x 2 = O	221 x 3 = V	112 x 4 = E
111 x 3 = E	413 x 2 = M	341 x 2 = T	314 x 2 = O	431 x 2 = T
322 x 3 = O	144 x 2 = S	414 x 2 = E	310 x 2 = T	323 x 2 = I

Why did Clarabell cross the road?

___ ___   ___ ___ ___   ___ ___
862 882   462 828 682   960 628

___ ___ ___   "___ ___ ___ - ___ ___ ___ ___"!
620 518 448   826 630 966   663 646 333 288

I had fun!

Trudy's Travel Troubles

Name _____   Date _____

Read.
Solve each problem on another sheet of paper.
Write the answer in the blank.

1. When Trudy visited Australia, she lost the candy mints she bought. She lost 111 mints each day for 8 days. How many mints did she lose in all?

   _____ mints

2. Trudy tried to make leis in Hawaii but damaged the flowers. She damaged 110 flowers each of the 6 days she was there. How many flowers did she damage in all?

   _____ flowers

3. Trudy liked drinking tea in England, but she had trouble holding the cups. She dropped 3 teacups each day for 101 days. How many teacups did she drop in all?

   _____ teacups

4. In France Trudy kept forgetting the names of famous artists. She forgot 112 names at 4 different art galleries. How many names did she forget in all?

   _____ names

5. In Egypt Trudy tripped on steps at the pyramids. She tripped 102 times at 4 different pyramids. How many times did she trip in all?

   _____ times

6. In Mexico Trudy sometimes spoke French instead of Spanish. She spoke French 211 times in 4 different towns. How many times did she speak French in all?

   _____ times

7. Trudy went skiing in Switzerland. She fell 9 times on each of the 100 days she was there. How many times did she fall in all?

   _____ times

Trouble follows me around!

Story problems: 3 digits x 1 digit without regrouping

Fancy Feathers

Name _____ Date _____

Multiply.
Color by the code.

3,441
x   2

4,234
x   2

2,033
x   3

2,021
x   4

3,102
x   3

1,243
x   2

2,413
x   2

1,223
x   3

2,331
x   3

3,034
x   2

1,312
x   3

1,234
x   2

1,012
x   4

4,321
x   2

3,343
x   2

3,231
x   3

Color Code
0–5,000 = green
5,001–10,000 = blue

2,112
x   4

2,124
x   2

1,313
x   3

Goin' Fishin'

Multiply.
Show your work on another sheet of paper.
Color each correct answer. Connect the colored boxes to draw a path to the fishing hole.

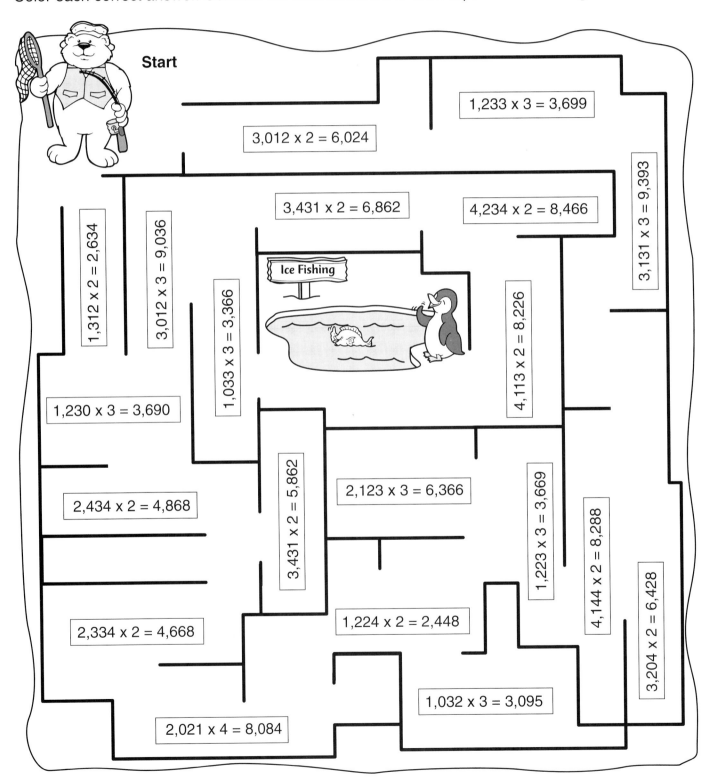

Start

1,233 x 3 = 3,699

3,012 x 2 = 6,024

3,431 x 2 = 6,862

4,234 x 2 = 8,466

3,131 x 3 = 9,393

1,312 x 2 = 2,634

3,012 x 3 = 9,036

1,033 x 3 = 3,366

Ice Fishing

4,113 x 2 = 8,226

1,230 x 3 = 3,690

2,434 x 2 = 4,868

3,431 x 2 = 5,862

2,123 x 3 = 6,366

1,223 x 3 = 3,669

4,144 x 2 = 8,288

3,204 x 2 = 6,428

2,334 x 2 = 4,668

1,224 x 2 = 2,448

1,032 x 3 = 3,095

2,021 x 4 = 8,084

Spotted Snacker

Name _____   Date _____

Multiply.
Show your work on another sheet of paper.
To solve the riddle, match the letters to the
  numbered lines below.

H   3,113 x 3 = _____

P   1,004 x 2 = _____

T   1,212 x 3 = _____

L   1,230 x 2 = _____

I   2,120 x 3 = _____

A   1,120 x 4 = _____

T   2,342 x 2 = _____

E   3,432 x 2 = _____

S   2,321 x 3 = _____

T   1,431 x 2 = _____

A   1,232 x 3 = _____

Y   1,432 x 2 = _____

E   2,123 x 3 = _____

H   2,332 x 3 = _____

T   4,123 x 2 = _____

L   1,223 x 2 = _____

H   1,231 x 3 = _____

T   1,033 x 3 = _____

O   2,120 x 4 = _____

R   3,023 x 3 = _____

What did the cheetah say after he finished his snack?

```
                              ____   ____   ____   ____
                              3,636  6,996  4,480  3,099

____   ____   ____   ____   ____   ____            ____   ____   ____
9,069  6,864  3,696  2,460  2,446  2,864           9,339  6,360  2,862
                                                                    ___!
       ____   ____   ____            ____   ____   ____   ____
       8,246  3,693  6,369           6,963  2,008  8,480  4,684
```

Sweet Shop

Name _____ Date _____

Read.
Solve each problem on another sheet of paper.
Write the answer in the blank.

TASTYTOWN Sweet Shop

1. The Tastytown Sweet Shop sells 2,412 chocolate pops each month. How many chocolate pops will the shop sell in 2 months?

   _____ chocolate pops

2. The Sweet Shop's owner orders 2,032 bags of jelly beans each year. In 3 years, how many bags of jelly beans will he have ordered in all?

   _____ bags

3. Each week the owner refills the gumball machine with 1,211 gumballs. How many gumballs will he put in the machine in 4 weeks?

   _____ gumballs

4. The Sweet Shop customers buy 3,123 fruit chews each month. How many fruit chews will customers buy in 3 months?

   _____ fruit chews

5. The Too Sweet Sugar Company delivers 1,021 pounds of sugar to the shop each week. After 4 weeks, how many pounds of sugar will they have delivered in all?

   _____ pounds

6. The workers at the shop made 4,432 pieces of candy last month. If they make the same amount of candy each month for 2 months, how many pieces of candy will they make in all?

   _____ pieces

Story problems: 4 digits x 1 digit without regrouping

Up, Up, and Away!

Date _____

Multiply.
Show your work.
Cross off each matching answer on the balloon.
Some numbers will not be crossed off.

Eek!

```
  24          29          18
x  4        x  3        x  5
____        ____        ____
```

```
  14          16          27
x  4        x  5        x  3
____        ____        ____
```

96

90

78   84   159

87

72

81   80

93

637   126

56

89

98   243

```
  49          13          91
x  2        x  6        x  7
____        ____        ____
```

```
  36          42          28
x  2        x  3        x  3
____        ____        ____
```

```
  81          53
x  3        x  3
____        ____
```

2 digits x 1 digit with one regrouping 19

Catching Anything?

Name _____ Date _____

Multiply.
Show your work.
Color each fish that has a matching answer.

27 x 3	18 x 5	13 x 6	90 x 5	21 x 7	41 x 5
72 x 4	35 x 2	14 x 6	38 x 2	83 x 3	25 x 3
46 x 2	93 x 3	28 x 2	16 x 6	91 x 9	32 x 4
40 x 5	61 x 4				

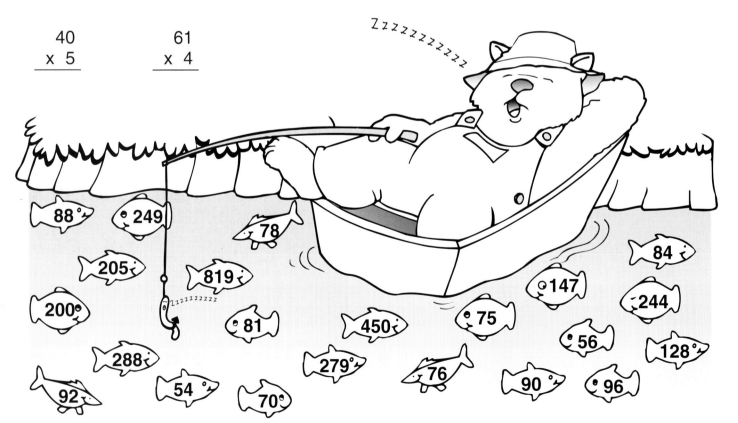

What's Wally Watching?

Name _____ Date _____

Multiply.
Show your work on another sheet of paper.
Color the boxes with correct answers to show the path to the TV show.

61 x 8 =	148	468	489	488
25 x 2 =	47	40	50	57
17 x 3 =	54	51	61	64
24 x 4 =	68	96	84	64
26 x 3 =	78	69	59	68
28 x 2 =	56	50	46	40
31 x 9 =	270	279	260	269
36 x 2 =	62	52	72	78
12 x 8 =	80	86	90	96
23 x 4 =	67	82	92	87
12 x 5 =	70	60	50	57
18 x 2 =	36	30	46	26
12 x 7 =	79	84	89	74
14 x 7 =	91	98	78	96
51 x 4 =	205	201	204	94
	Walrus World	Tips on Tusks	100 Ways to Eat Clams	Ice Floe Tricks

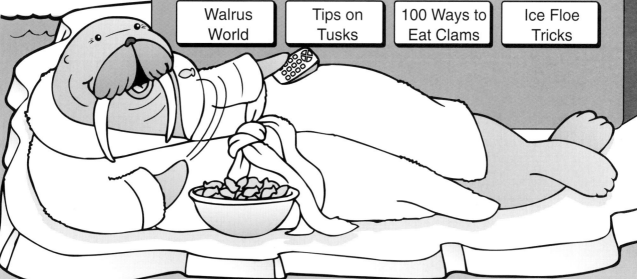

2 digits x 1 digit with one regrouping 21

Such Silly Seals!

Name _____   Date _____

Read.
Solve each problem on another sheet of paper.
Write the answer in the blank.

1. Sammy and Susie Seal perform silly shows. If they ride bikes in 2 shows each day for the next 27 weeks, in how many shows will they ride bikes in all?

_____ shows

2. Susie Seal juggles fish toys while riding a skateboard. If she juggles 5 toys in 16 different shows, how many toys will she juggle in all?

_____ toys

3. Sammy blows up beach balls for their act. If, over the next 17 weeks, Susie pops 4 balls each week, how many balls will pop in all?

_____ balls

4. At 15 different shows, 6 people each wanted to take a picture of Susie. If Susie crosses her eyes in the pictures, how many people in all will get cross-eyed pictures?

_____ people

5. While Sammy balances a beach ball on his nose, he stands on one front flipper and juggles fish toys in the other. If he does this for 5 minutes in each of 14 shows, how long will he balance in all?

_____ minutes

6. Sammy also twirls plastic hoops around his neck while he sings "Yankee Doodle." If he twirls 4 hoops at a time in each of 16 shows, how many hoops will he twirl in all?

_____ hoops

Story problems: 2 digits x 1 digit with one regrouping

Fresh From the Honeycomb

Name _____ Date _____

Multiply.
Show your work.

307
x 2

219
x 4

127
x 3

324
x 3

245
x 2

141
x 5

128
x 3

253
x 2

315
x 2

192
x 4

120
x 8

116
x 6

346
x 2

263
x 3

3 digits x 1 digit with one regrouping

Just Like Home!

Name _____ Date _____

Multiply.
Show your work.
To solve the riddle, match the letters to the numbered lines below.

```
  108
x   5
_____
      = E
```

```
  446
x   2
_____
      = O
```

```
  118
x   3
_____
      = R
```

```
  218
x   4
_____
      = O
```

```
  306
x   2
_____
      = A
```

```
  140
x   6
_____
      = V
```

```
  291
x   3
_____
      = I
```

```
  107
x   6
_____
      = T
```

```
  153
x   3
_____
      = G
```

```
  482
x   2
_____
      = M
```

```
  339
x   2
_____
      = L
```

```
  105
x   7
_____
      = R
```

```
  328
x   3
_____
      = H
```

```
  260
x   3
_____
      = P
```

```
  214
x   4
_____
      = E
```

```
  217
x   4
_____
      = H
```

```
  381
x   2
_____
      = E
```

```
  104
x   4
_____
      = T
```

Where did the baseball player pitch his tent?

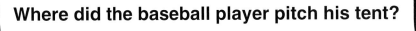

```
___  ___  ___  ___  ___
354  873  459  984  642

___  ___  ___  ___
872  840  856  735

___  ___  ___  ___
868  892  964  762

___  ___  ___  ___  ___ !
780  678  612  416  540
```

3 digits x 1 digit with one regrouping

Help Me Down!

Name _____ Date _____

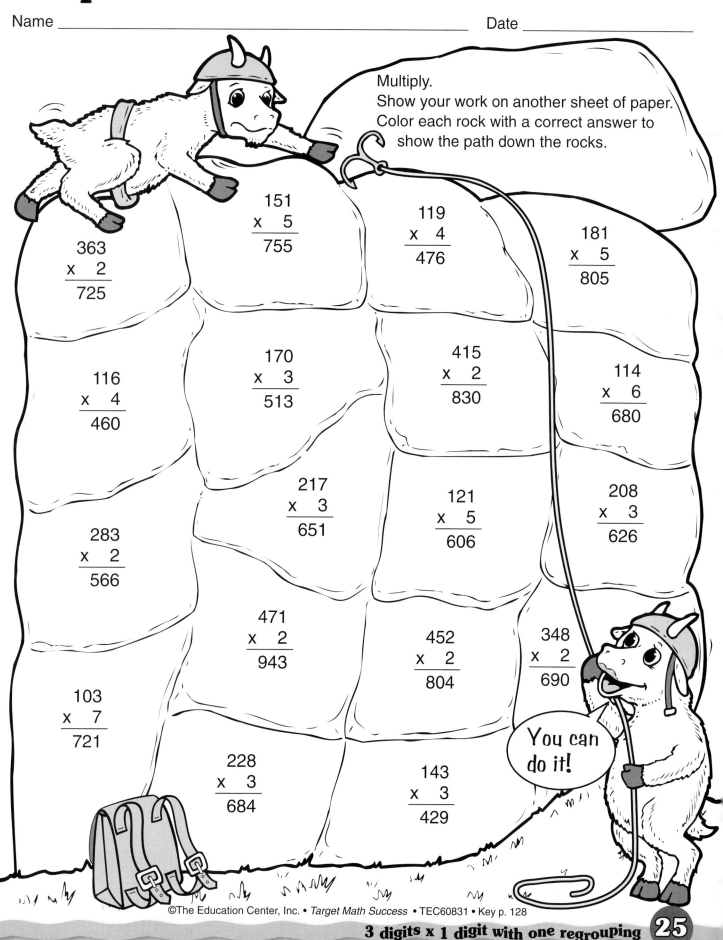

Multiply.
Show your work on another sheet of paper.
Color each rock with a correct answer to show the path down the rocks.

151
x 5
755

119
x 4
476

181
x 5
805

363
x 2
725

116
x 4
460

170
x 3
513

415
x 2
830

114
x 6
680

283
x 2
566

217
x 3
651

121
x 5
606

208
x 3
626

103
x 7
721

471
x 2
943

452
x 2
804

348
x 2
690

228
x 3
684

143
x 3
429

You can do it!

3 digits x 1 digit with one regrouping

Ellie's Jungle Mart

Name _____ Date _____

Read.
Solve each problem on another sheet of paper.
Write the answer in the blank.

1. Ellie stocked 2 shelves with tree branches. She put 105 branches on each shelf. How many branches did she stock in all?

_____ branches

2. There are 3 shelves for strips of bark. Each shelf holds 282 strips. How many strips of bark will the shelves hold in all?

_____ strips of bark

3. Sugarcane bundles are on sale. Ellie sold 113 bundles. Each bundle holds 6 sugarcane stalks. How many stalks did Ellie sell in all?

_____ stalks

4. Today 224 elephants came through Ellie's express lane. Each elephant bought 4 items. How many total items were sold to elephants in the express lane today?

_____ items

5. One case of coconuts holds 8. Ellie moved 121 cases. How many coconuts did she move in all?

_____ coconuts

6. If Ellie sells 191 gallons of milk each week, how many gallons of milk will she sell in 5 weeks?

_____ gallons of milk

Story problems: 3 digits x 1 digit with one regrouping

Zoom, Zoom, Zoom!

Name _____ Date _____

Multiply.
Show your work.
Color each matching answer on the racetrack.

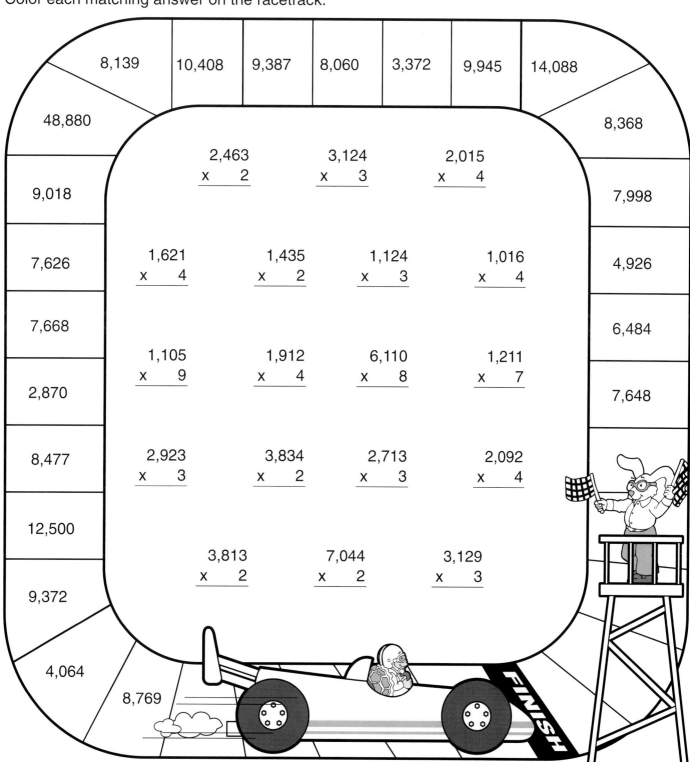

| 8,139 | 10,408 | 9,387 | 8,060 | 3,372 | 9,945 | 14,088 |

48,880

8,368

9,018

| 2,463 | 3,124 | 2,015 |
| x 2 | x 3 | x 4 |

7,998

7,626

| 1,621 | 1,435 | 1,124 | 1,016 |
| x 4 | x 2 | x 3 | x 4 |

4,926

7,668

6,484

| 1,105 | 1,912 | 6,110 | 1,211 |
| x 9 | x 4 | x 8 | x 7 |

2,870

7,648

8,477

| 2,923 | 3,834 | 2,713 | 2,092 |
| x 3 | x 2 | x 3 | x 4 |

12,500

| 3,813 | 7,044 | 3,129 |
| x 2 | x 2 | x 3 |

9,372

4,064

8,769

Where's All the Booty Buried?

Name _____   Date _____

Multiply.
Show your work on another sheet of paper.
If correct, color the island green.
If incorrect, color the island blue.
The treasure is on the green islands.

$$1,103 \times 6 = 6,618$$

$$1,307 \times 3 = 3,921$$

$$2,194 \times 2 = 4,386$$

$$1,181 \times 4 = 4,724$$

$$2,216 \times 4 = 8,864$$

$$3,439 \times 2 = 6,878$$

$$1,416 \times 2 = 2,722$$

$$3,110 \times 8 = 24,880$$

$$3,372 \times 2 = 5,644$$

$$2,402 \times 3 = 7,206$$

$$1,091 \times 6 = 6,546$$

$$1,812 \times 4 = 7,446$$

$$3,513 \times 2 = 7,026$$

$$1,006 \times 6 = 6,036$$

$$6,001 \times 7 = 42,007$$

$$1,031 \times 5 = 5,055$$

©The Education Center, Inc. • *Target Math Success* • TEC60831 • Key p. 128

28 **4 digits x 1 digit with one regrouping**

Aim for the Green!

Name _____ Date _____

Multiply.
Show your work.
Cross off the matching answer on the trees.
Some numbers will not be crossed off.

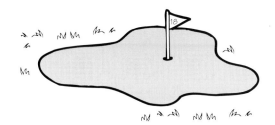

$$\begin{array}{r} 1,013 \\ \times\ \ \ 7 \\ \hline \end{array} \qquad \begin{array}{r} 1,210 \\ \times\ \ \ 8 \\ \hline \end{array}$$

$$\begin{array}{r} 2,252 \\ \times\ \ \ 3 \\ \hline \end{array} \qquad \begin{array}{r} 1,921 \\ \times\ \ \ 4 \\ \hline \end{array} \qquad \begin{array}{r} 1,500 \\ \times\ \ \ 6 \\ \hline \end{array} \qquad \begin{array}{r} 2,162 \\ \times\ \ \ 3 \\ \hline \end{array}$$

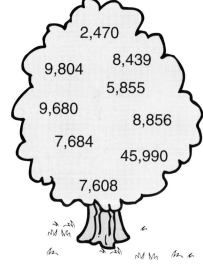

2,470
8,439
9,804
5,855
9,680
8,856
7,684
45,990
7,608

$$\begin{array}{r} 1,305 \\ \times\ \ \ 3 \\ \hline \end{array} \qquad \begin{array}{r} 1,171 \\ \times\ \ \ 5 \\ \hline \end{array} \qquad \begin{array}{r} 5,110 \\ \times\ \ \ 9 \\ \hline \end{array} \qquad \begin{array}{r} 1,107 \\ \times\ \ \ 8 \\ \hline \end{array}$$

$$\begin{array}{r} 1,140 \\ \times\ \ \ 7 \\ \hline \end{array} \qquad \begin{array}{r} 1,235 \\ \times\ \ \ 2 \\ \hline \end{array} \qquad \begin{array}{r} 9,011 \\ \times\ \ \ 6 \\ \hline \end{array} \qquad \begin{array}{r} 1,106 \\ \times\ \ \ 8 \\ \hline \end{array}$$

$$\begin{array}{r} 2,813 \\ \times\ \ \ 3 \\ \hline \end{array} \qquad \begin{array}{r} 4,902 \\ \times\ \ \ 2 \\ \hline \end{array} \qquad \begin{array}{r} 2,215 \\ \times\ \ \ 4 \\ \hline \end{array}$$

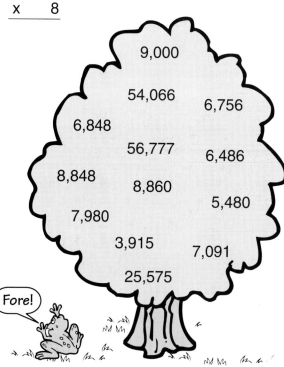

9,000
54,066
6,756
6,848
56,777
6,486
8,848
8,860
5,480
7,980
3,915
7,091
25,575

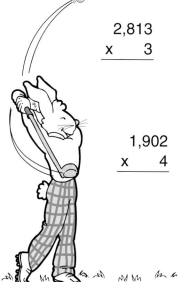

$$\begin{array}{r} 1,902 \\ \times\ \ \ 4 \\ \hline \end{array} \qquad \begin{array}{r} 8,111 \\ \times\ \ \ 7 \\ \hline \end{array} \qquad \begin{array}{r} 1,712 \\ \times\ \ \ 4 \\ \hline \end{array}$$

Fore!

Got Plumbing Problems?

Name _____ Date _____

Read.
Solve each problem on another sheet of paper.
Write the answer in the blank.
To solve the riddle, write the letter of each answer in its matching numbered blank below.

1. The Lily Pad plumbers are busy. They fixed 1,018 broken pipes last month. At this rate, how many pipes will these plumbers fix in 3 months?

    _____ pipes = O

2. Drippy faucets are also a big problem. The plumbers fixed 1,160 of them last month. At this rate, how many drippy faucets will the plumbers fix in 6 months?

    _____ faucets = C

3. Another problem is stopped-up drains. The plumbers repaired 1,106 of them last month. At this rate, how many drains will the plumbers repair in 9 months?

    _____ drains = L

4. Some folks want the plumbers to put in new water heaters. If the plumbers put in 1,253 heaters each month, how many will they put in in 2 months?

    _____ water heaters = S

5. Other folks need new water pumps. If the plumbers put in 1,004 pumps each month, how many will they install in 8 months?

    _____ pumps = G

What kind of shoes do plumbers never wear?

___ ___ ___ ___ ___!
6,960 9,954 3,054 8,032 2,506

Story problems: 4 digits x 1 digit with one regrouping

Paint Job

Name _____   Date _____

Multiply.
Show your work.
Color by the code.

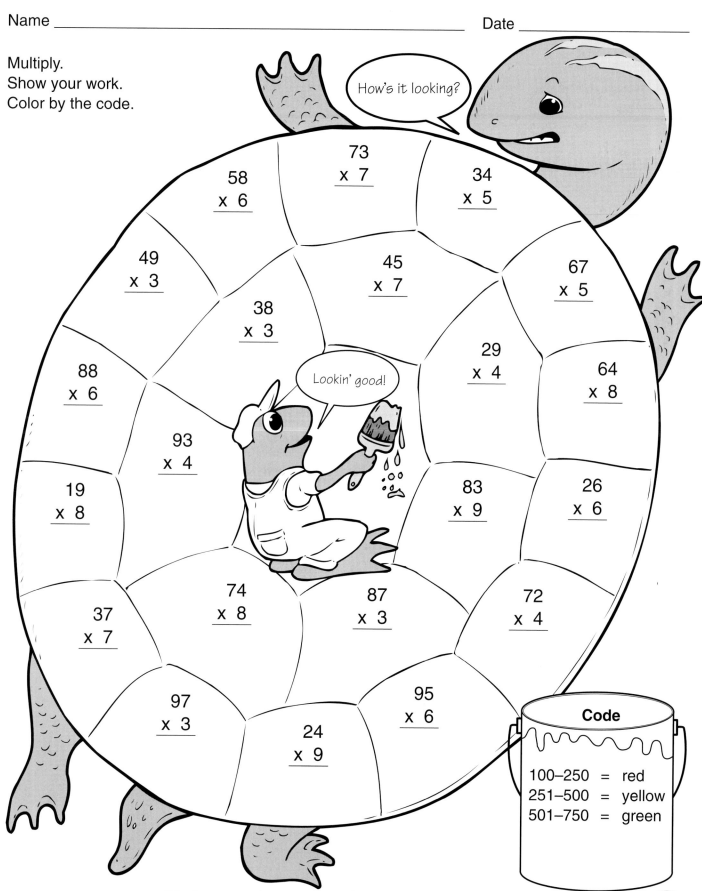

How's it looking?

Lookin' good!

73
x 7

58
x 6

34
x 5

49
x 3

45
x 7

67
x 5

38
x 3

29
x 4

64
x 8

88
x 6

93
x 4

83
x 9

26
x 6

19
x 8

74
x 8

87
x 3

72
x 4

37
x 7

97
x 3

24
x 9

95
x 6

Code

100–250 = red
251–500 = yellow
501–750 = green

All Ears!

Name _____   Date _____

Multiply.
Show your work.
Write each answer in the square below. The sum of each row and column should be 1,000.

1. 48
    x 3

2. 62
    x 5

3. 56
    x 4

4. 46
    x 7

5. 72
    x 7

6. 39
    x 5

7. 37
    x 3

8. 38
    x 5

9. 19
    x 8

10. 37
     x 9

11. 45
     x 9

12. 22
     x 5

13. 25
     x 8

14. 18
     x 9

15. 52
     x 5

16. 63
     x 6

1.	2.	3.	4.
5.	6.	7.	8.
9.	10.	11.	12.
13.	14.	15.	16.

Got Ya!

Name _____ Date _____

Multiply.
Show your work.
Cross off each answer on the boots.
Some numbers will not be crossed off.

17	27	33	74	39
x 8	x 5	x 4	x 3	x 8

46	24	54	65	69
x 6	x 7	x 5	x 7	x 3

77	57	48	55	82
x 7	x 4	x 4	x 7	x 9

94	44	16	81	92
x 3	x 5	x 9	x 8	x 6

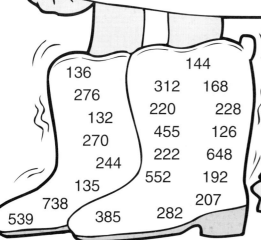

136
276
132
270
244
135
738
539

144
312   168
220   228
455   126
222   648
552   192
207
385   282

Beep! Beep!

Name _____ Date _____

Multiply.
Show your work on another sheet of paper.

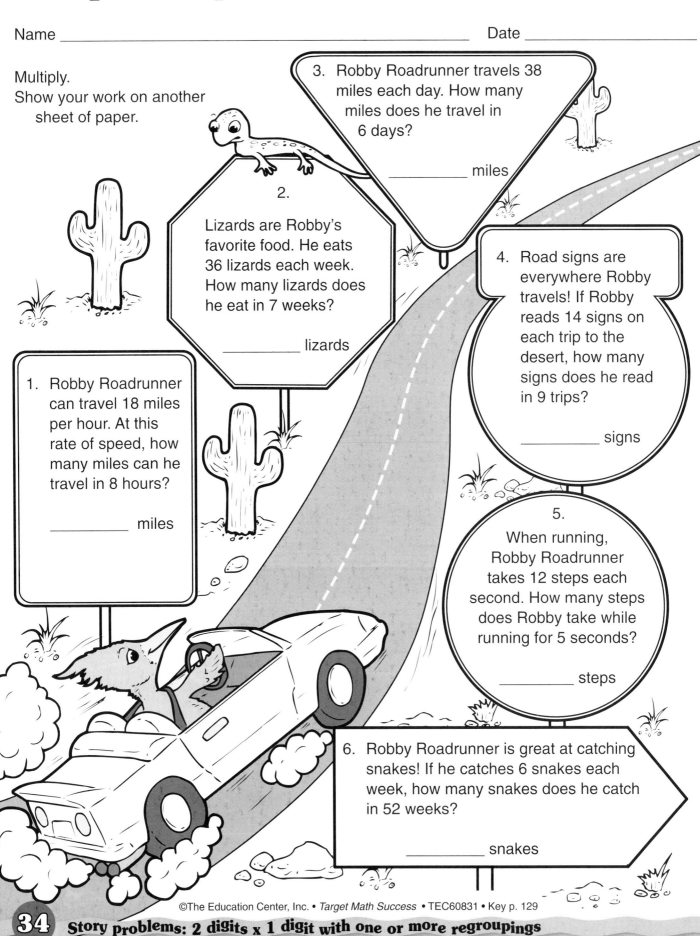

3. Robby Roadrunner travels 38 miles each day. How many miles does he travel in 6 days?

_____ miles

2. Lizards are Robby's favorite food. He eats 36 lizards each week. How many lizards does he eat in 7 weeks?

_____ lizards

4. Road signs are everywhere Robby travels! If Robby reads 14 signs on each trip to the desert, how many signs does he read in 9 trips?

_____ signs

1. Robby Roadrunner can travel 18 miles per hour. At this rate of speed, how many miles can he travel in 8 hours?

_____ miles

5. When running, Robby Roadrunner takes 12 steps each second. How many steps does Robby take while running for 5 seconds?

_____ steps

6. Robby Roadrunner is great at catching snakes! If he catches 6 snakes each week, how many snakes does he catch in 52 weeks?

_____ snakes

Story problems: 2 digits x 1 digit with one or more regroupings

What's the Very Important Date?

Name _____   Date _____

Multiply.

Show your work.

To show the path to the event, color the clocks whose answers end in **5, 6,** or **8**.

You're late! You're late!

Yikes!

655 x 7	897 x 8	346 x 4
583 x 4	728 x 9	319 x 6	279 x 5
426 x 7	684 x 3	867 x 4	538 x 3
764 x 5	296 x 8	393 x 4	817 x 9

eat carrot soup with Alice

play cards with the Queen of Hearts

buy a hat for the Mad Hatter

take catnip to the Cheshire Cat

©The Education Center, Inc. • *Target Math Success* • TEC60831 • Key p. 129

3 digits x 1 digit with one or more regroupings 35

Football Fever!

Name _____   Date _____

Multiply.
Show your work on another sheet of paper.
Color if correct.
Connect the colored footballs to show the path to the goal.

Go Bulldogs!

Start

$$\begin{array}{r} 663 \\ \times\ \ 7 \\ \hline 4{,}641 \end{array}$$

$$\begin{array}{r} 817 \\ \times\ \ 9 \\ \hline 7{,}353 \end{array}$$

$$\begin{array}{r} 264 \\ \times\ \ 5 \\ \hline 1{,}800 \end{array}$$

40

$$\begin{array}{r} 492 \\ \times\ \ 6 \\ \hline 2{,}942 \end{array}$$

$$\begin{array}{r} 198 \\ \times\ \ 3 \\ \hline 394 \end{array}$$

$$\begin{array}{r} 232 \\ \times\ \ 8 \\ \hline 1{,}856 \end{array}$$

$$\begin{array}{r} 615 \\ \times\ \ 7 \\ \hline 4{,}335 \end{array}$$

30

$$\begin{array}{r} 569 \\ \times\ \ 2 \\ \hline 1{,}038 \end{array}$$

$$\begin{array}{r} 337 \\ \times\ \ 4 \\ \hline 1{,}328 \end{array}$$

$$\begin{array}{r} 767 \\ \times\ \ 7 \\ \hline 5{,}469 \end{array}$$

$$\begin{array}{r} 168 \\ \times\ \ 5 \\ \hline 840 \end{array}$$

20

$$\begin{array}{r} 693 \\ \times\ \ 8 \\ \hline 5{,}524 \end{array}$$

$$\begin{array}{r} 495 \\ \times\ \ 2 \\ \hline 890 \end{array}$$

$$\begin{array}{r} 358 \\ \times\ \ 4 \\ \hline 1{,}432 \end{array}$$

$$\begin{array}{r} 759 \\ \times\ \ 9 \\ \hline 6{,}731 \end{array}$$

10

A 40-yard touchdown!

TOUCH-DOWN!

Run!

COACH

3 digits x 1 digit with one or more regroupings

Tooth Alert!

Name _____ Date _____

Multiply.
Show your work on another sheet of paper.
Color by the code to solve the riddle.

Color Code

Answer starting with 3–9 = yellow

Answer starting with 2 = blue

Answer starting with 1 = red

What two letters are bad for your teeth?

397
x   9

523
x   7

289
x   3

814
x   8

656
x   8

189
x   6

488
x   4

564
x   6

824
x   6

246 x 8 =

676 x 2 =

984
x   5

693
x   5

373
x   5

934
x   5

757
x   9

537
x   3

639
x   5

828
x   4

862
x   7

755
x   4

483
x   5

366
x   9

385 x 6 =

729 x 4 =

834 x 3 =

555
x   5

358
x   7

Roscoe's Roundup!

Name _____ Date _____

Read.
Solve each problem on another sheet of paper.
Write the answer in the blank.
To solve the riddle, write the letter of each answer
in its matching numbered blank below.

Head 'em up and move 'em out!

1. The cowboys at Roscoe's ranch will round up 167 horses each day for 6 days. How many horses will the cowboys round up in all?

   _____ horses (C)

2. The horses will be rounded up from 5 different pastures. If there are 225 acres in each pasture, how many acres of pasture are there in all?

   _____ acres (R)

3. The cowboys will round up cows from 7 different pastures. If there are 364 cows in each pasture, how many cows will be rounded up in all?

   _____ cows (N)

4. Roscoe's ranch hands will round up calves from 3 different pastures. If there are 454 calves in each pasture, how many calves will be rounded up in all?

   _____ calves (T)

5. Roscoe has the cowboys store hay in 9 different barns. If each barn holds 856 bales of hay, how many bales are stored in all?

   _____ bales (O)

6. Oats are stored in 4 different bins. If each bin holds 645 pounds of oats, how many pounds are stored in all?

   _____ pounds (B)

What disease did Roscoe get after trying to break a wild horse?

" _____ _____ _____ _____ - I ____ I S "!
2,580   1,125   7,704   2,548   1,002   1,362

Story problems: 3 digits x 1 digit with one or more regroupings

Beach Blanket

Name _____ Date _____

Multiply.
Show your work.
Color by the code.

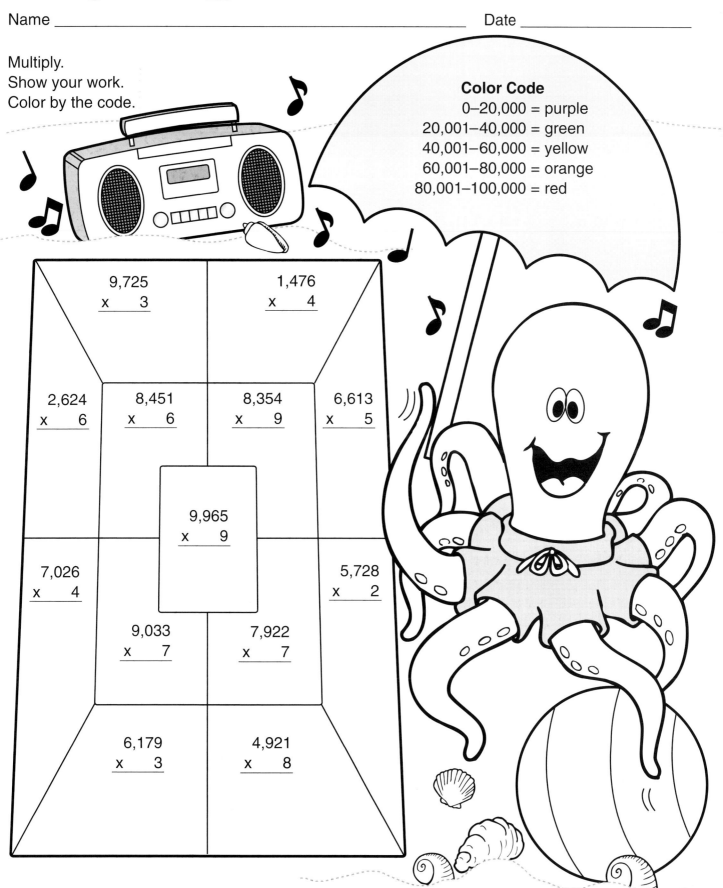

Color Code
0–20,000 = purple
20,001–40,000 = green
40,001–60,000 = yellow
60,001–80,000 = orange
80,001–100,000 = red

9,725 x 3	1,476 x 4

2,624 x 6	8,451 x 6	8,354 x 9	6,613 x 5

9,965
x   9

7,026 x 4	5,728 x 2

9,033 x 7	7,922 x 7

6,179 x 3	4,921 x 8

Pencil Pals

Name _____ Date _____

Multiply.
Show your work on another sheet of paper.
Match the letters to the numbered lines below to solve the riddle.

O   3,603 x 4 = _____

S   9,562 x 7 = _____

D   2,128 x 6 = _____

U   8,402 x 5 = _____

L   4,529 x 8 = _____

A   6,223 x 9 = _____

O   7,164 x 2 = _____

H   5,729 x 3 = _____

K   2,170 x 5 = _____

Y   9,626 x 4 = _____

P   8,719 x 9 = _____

A   1,783 x 8 = _____

O   6,423 x 6 = _____

T   3,431 x 7 = _____

R   5,023 x 4 = _____

O   4,196 x 3 = _____

Y   4,735 x 4 = _____

What did one pencil say to the other pencil?

___ ___ ___   ___ ___ ___ ___
38,504 14,328 42,010   36,232 38,538 12,588 10,850

___ ___ ___ ___ ___
66,934 17,187 14,264 20,092 78,471

___ ___ ___ ___ ___ !
24,017 14,412 12,768 56,007 18,940

4 digits x 1 digit with one or more regroupings

Route to the Loot

Name _____   Date _____

Multiply.
Show your work on another sheet of paper.
Color if correct.
Connect the colored boxes to draw a path
   to the treasure chest.

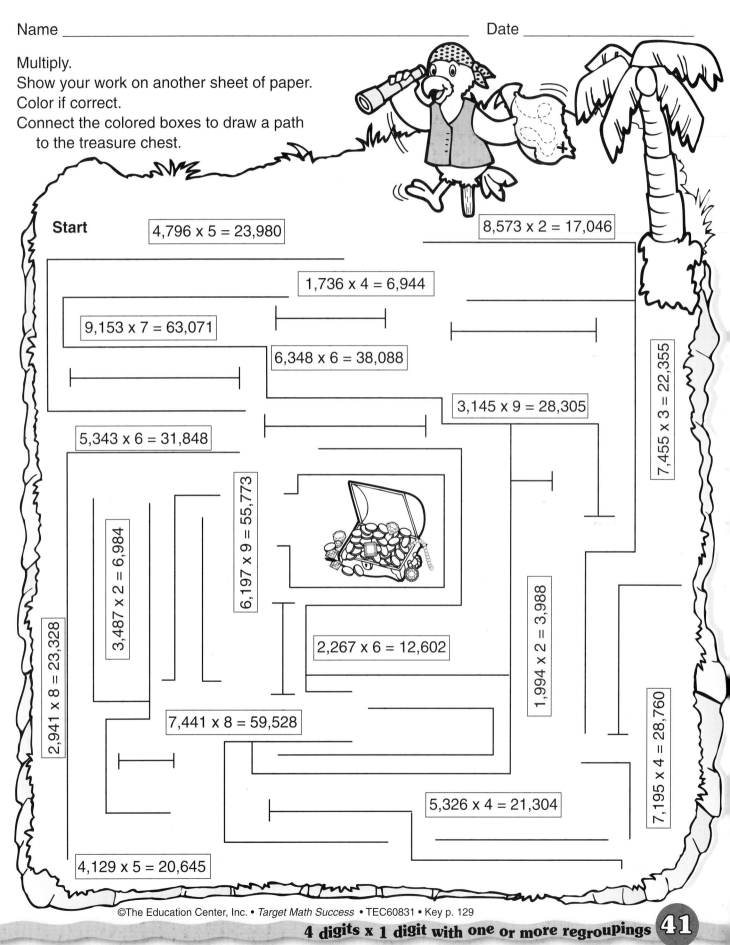

Start

4,796 x 5 = 23,980

8,573 x 2 = 17,046

1,736 x 4 = 6,944

9,153 x 7 = 63,071

6,348 x 6 = 38,088

3,145 x 9 = 28,305

7,455 x 3 = 22,355

5,343 x 6 = 31,848

6,197 x 9 = 55,773

3,487 x 2 = 6,984

2,941 x 8 = 23,328

2,267 x 6 = 12,602

1,994 x 2 = 3,988

7,195 x 4 = 28,760

7,441 x 8 = 59,528

5,326 x 4 = 21,304

4,129 x 5 = 20,645

4 digits x 1 digit with one or more regroupings

On the Go

Name _____ Date _____

Read.
Solve each problem on another sheet of paper.
Write the answer in the blank.

1. If 4,178 planes fly each day, how many planes will fly in 3 days?

_____ planes

2. If 2,275 people sail on each cruise ship, how many people will sail on 8 cruise ships?

_____ people

3. If 3,872 people use the subway each day, how many people will use the subway in 5 days?

_____ people

4. If a truck driver drives 1,986 miles on each trip, how many miles will he drive in 9 trips?

_____ miles

5. If 7,135 cars travel on the road each month, how many cars will travel on the road in 4 months?

_____ cars

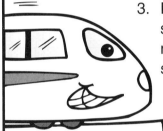

6. If 1,863 bikes travel on the trail each month, how many bikes will travel on the trail in 2 months?

_____ bikes

7. If 6,589 people ride the bus each week, how many people will ride the bus in 6 weeks?

_____ people

8. If a train travels 5,298 miles each week, how many miles will the train travel in 7 weeks?

_____ miles

Who's Minding the Castle?

Name _____   Date _____

Multiply.
Show your work.
Cross off the matching answer on the castle door.
Some numbers will not be crossed off.

31	13	17	42	21
x 23	x 13	x 11	x 20	x 14

	37	14	41	33
	x 11	x 12	x 12	x 13

	32	40
	x 21	x 22

	34	29
	x 21	x 11

169	714
319	407
429	112
850	840
713	187
880	294
168	492
672	

One-Stop Shopping

Name _____   Date _____

Multiply.
Show your work on another sheet of paper.
Color boxes with correct answers to show the path to the outlet.

	18 x 10 180	44 x 22 968	23 x 12 276

Start

32 x 31 992	75 x 11 825	16 x 10 170	34 x 22 746	32 x 13 415	43 x 20 860
51 x 11 561	42 x 21 881	24 x 21 504	43 x 12 516	33 x 23 759	19 x 11 209
40 x 20 800	37 x 11 517	62 x 10 730			
86 x 11 947	44 x 12 528	70 x 10 700			

Bamboo Outlet

Finish

Room for One More?

Name _____ Date _____

Multiply.
Show your work on another sheet of paper.
Color by the code.

Color Code
100–300 = orange
301–600 = green
601–900 = red
901–1,000 = blue

34
x 20

23
x 23

24
x 12

31
x 13

44
x 21

17
x 10

87
x 11

33
x 22

19
x 11

13
x 11

22
x 14

41
x 21

Way Cool Music

Name _____ Date _____

Read.
Solve each problem on another sheet of paper.
Write the answer in the blank.

1.

I. C. Ice made 14 CDs.
Each CD has 21 songs.
How many songs are
there in all?

_____ songs

2.

I. C. wrote 22 songs for his
last CD. He spent 43 minutes
writing each song. How many
minutes did it take I. C. to
write the songs in all?

_____ minutes

3.

I. C. ordered 31 cartons of
T-shirts to give away at his
first concert. Each carton
has 12 shirts. How many
shirts will he give away
in all?

_____ shirts

4.

I. C. will visit 11 music
stores to promote his new
CD. He has agreed to sign
35 autographs at each store.
How many autographs will he
sign in all?

_____ autographs

5.

I. C.'s concert is sold out! A
ticket was sold for every seat.
There are 44 rows of seats. Each
row has 20 seats. How many
tickets were sold
to I. C.'s concert?

_____ tickets

I. C. Ice

SOLD OUT!

6.

I. C. and his group drink
13 bottles of water at every
concert. They have 23 concerts.
How many bottles of water will
they need?

_____ bottles of water

Snake in the Grass

Name _____   Date _____

Multiply.
Show your work.
Color by the code.

Color Code
0–3,000 = red
3,001–6,000 = yellow
6,001–9,000 = gray
9,001–12,000 = green

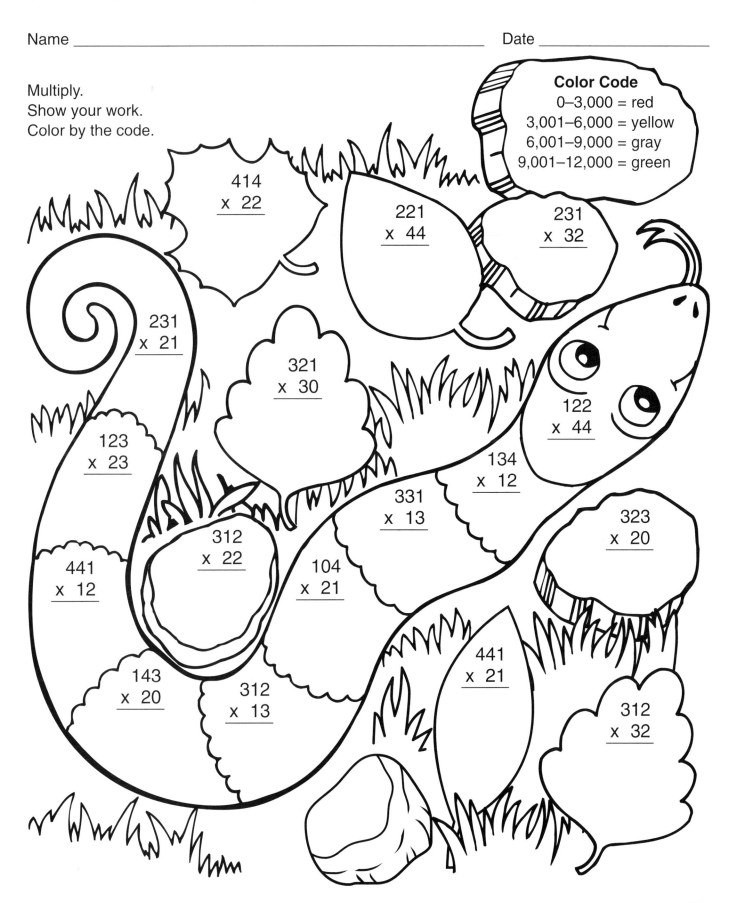

414
x 22

221
x 44

231
x 32

231
x 21

321
x 30

122
x 44

123
x 23

134
x 12

331
x 13

323
x 20

312
x 22

104
x 21

441
x 12

143
x 20

312
x 13

441
x 21

312
x 32

3 digits x 2 digits without regrouping

And the Winner Is...

Name _____ Date _____

Multiply.
Show your work on another sheet of paper.
Color to show the path
  to the winner's ribbon.

Big Race Today!

	IMPALA	JAGUAR	PANTHER	LION
123 x 32 =	3,906	3,935	4,036	3,936
414 x 21 =	6,694	8,794	8,694	8,674
321 x 33 =	10,583	10,593	10,603	10,493
104 x 22 =	2,308	2,286	2,288	2,388
313 x 23 =	7,189	7,199	7,209	7,196
134 x 20 =	2,680	3,680	2,660	2,580
312 x 31 =	9,672	6,672	9,662	9,682
323 x 30 =	9,693	9,690	9,660	9,590
221 x 42 =	9,082	7,282	9,282	9,292
143 x 12 =	1,616	1,715	1,696	1,716
241 x 21 =	5,062	4,861	5,061	4,061
421 x 22 =	9,272	8,262	9,262	9,062
122 x 31 =	3,672	3,782	4,782	3,793
330 x 32 =	10,450	10,560	10,562	10,260
112 x 43 =	4,816	4,796	4,926	4,916

IMPALA   JAGUAR   PANTHER   LION

3 digits x 2 digits without regrouping

The Buzz About Baseball

Name _____ Date _____

Multiply.
Show your work on another sheet of paper.
Color each space that contains a correct answer.

Buzzzzz

143 x 21 =   123 x 31 =   130 x 33 =

412 x 22 =   331 x 33 =   212 x 13 =

130 x 31 =   312 x 12 =   123 x 23 =

121 x 14 =   241 x 22 =   134 x 21 =

313 x 13 =   323 x 31 =   222 x 41 =

441 x 22 =   421 x 20 =   331 x 12 =

What kind of baseball has wings and six legs?

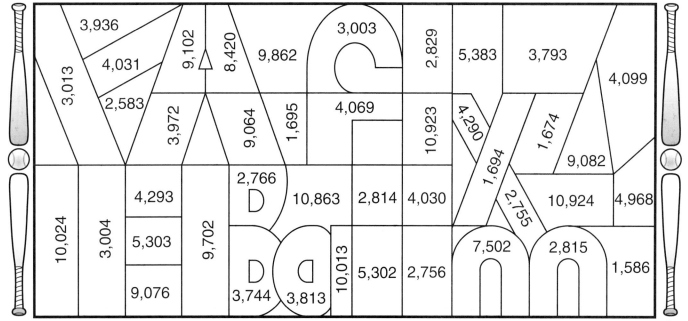

Tasty Treats

Read.
Solve each problem on another sheet of paper.
Write your answer in the blank.

1. Yesterday the baker at Fresh-From-the-Oven Bakery made 384 doughnuts. If he makes the same amount each day for 11 days, how many doughnuts will he make in all?

   _____ doughnuts

   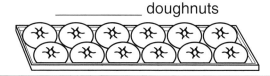

2. Last week the bakery sold 143 sticky buns. If the bakery sells the same amount each week for 22 weeks, how many sticky buns will be sold in all?

   _____ sticky buns

3. This week Easy-Bake Flour Company delivered 443 pounds of flour to the bakery. If the same amount is delivered each week for 21 weeks, how many pounds of flour will be delivered in all?

   _____ pounds

4. This month the bakery received 210 orders for birthday cakes. If the bakery receives the same number of orders each month for 14 months, how many orders will be received in all?

   _____ orders

   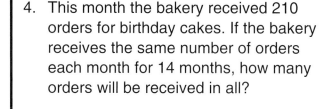

5. Last week the baker made 102 loaves of bread. If he makes the same number of loaves each week for 42 weeks, how many loaves will he bake in all?

   _____ loaves

6. Last month the bakery sold 314 pies. If the bakery sells the same number of pies each month for 12 months, how many pies will be sold in all?

   _____ pies

Story problems: 3 digits x 2 digits without regrouping

Floating on Cloud Nine

Name _____   Date _____

Multiply.
Show your work.
To solve the riddle, write the letter of each answer in its matching
numbered blank below.

Cloud Nine

1,434
x   22

S

4,113
x   12

Y

6,894
x   11

T

2,304
x   21

E

3,012
x   32

T

1,301
x   33

U

1,220
x   43

B

2,021
x   14

E

Who put Billy Bob on Cloud Nine?

_____ _____ _____ _____ _____   _____ _____ _____
52,460 48,384 75,834 96,384 49,356   31,548 42,933 28,294

Lighting the Way

Name _____   Date _____

Multiply.
Show your work.
Color the matching street lamp.

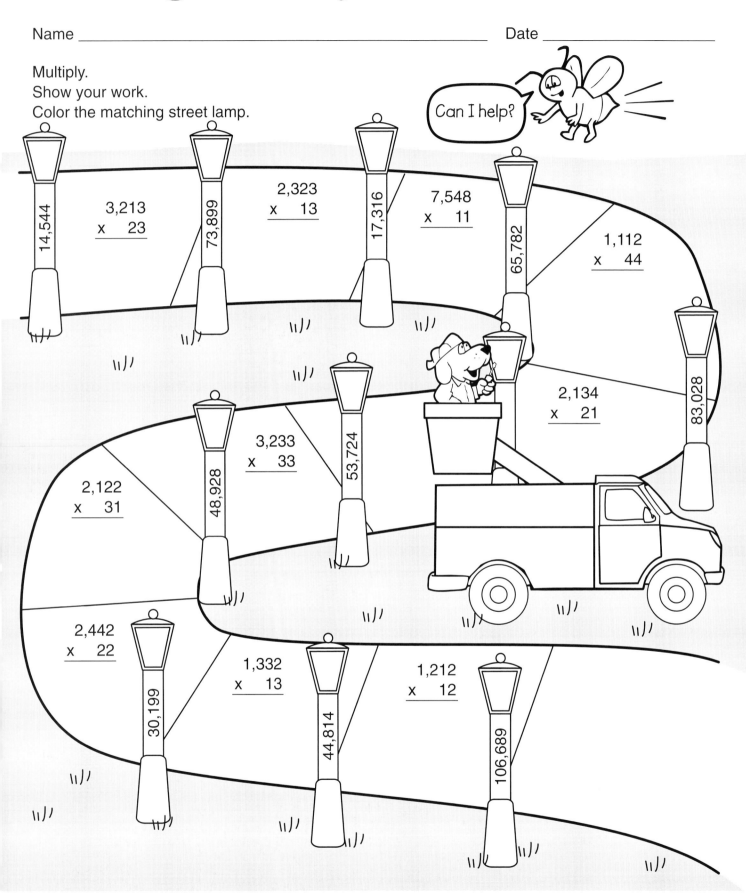

Can I help?

14,544

3,213
x   23

73,899

2,323
x   13

17,316

7,548
x   11

65,782

1,112
x   44

83,028

2,134
x   21

2,122
x   31

48,928

3,233
x   33

53,724

2,442
x   22

30,199

1,332
x   13

44,814

1,212
x   12

106,689

4 digits x 2 digits without regrouping

Cornfield Conversation

Name _____   Date _____

Multiply.
Show your work on another sheet of paper.
To solve the riddle, match the letters on the husks to the numbered blanks below.
Some letters will not be used.

2,131
x   32

A

1,133
x   22

S

2,233
x   13

H

8,754
x   11

U

3,131
x   32

C

2,013
x   11

K

3,331
x   12

T

1,331
x   12

O

1,442
x   21

Y

What kind of dog could hide easily in a cornfield?

68,192

" _____ _____ _____ _____ - _____ " !
  29,029   96,294   24,926   22,143   30,282

Meet the Rock Hounds!

Name _____   Date _____

Read.
Solve each problem on another sheet of paper.
Write the answer in the blank.

1.
The Rock Hounds have 3,102 tickets to sell for a show. If the band sells this number of tickets for 32 shows, how many tickets will it sell in all?

_____ tickets

2.
After one show, 4,321 fans asked for autographed pictures. If the band gets this number of requests at 11 shows, how many requests will it get in all?

_____ requests

3.
A radio station got 1,043 requests in one week for the band's newest song. At this rate, how many requests for that song will the station get in 21 weeks?

_____ requests

4.
The group got 2,110 requests for Rock Hound T-shirts in one day. If the group gets this many requests for 31 days, how many requests will it get in all?

_____ requests

5.
The Rock Hounds traveled 1,122 miles last month. If the group travels that number of miles during each of 14 months, how many miles will it travel in all?

_____ miles

6.
Fans give stuffed animals to the band members. During the last tour, they got 2,303 stuffed animals. If the band gets this number on each of 13 different tours, how many stuffed animals will it have in all?

_____ stuffed animals

©The Education Center, Inc. • *Target Math Success* • TEC60831 • Key p. 131

Story problems: 4 digits x 2 digits without regrouping

Fishin' for a Big One

Name _____   Date _____

Multiply.
Show your work.
Cross off each answer on the whale.
Some numbers will not be crossed off.

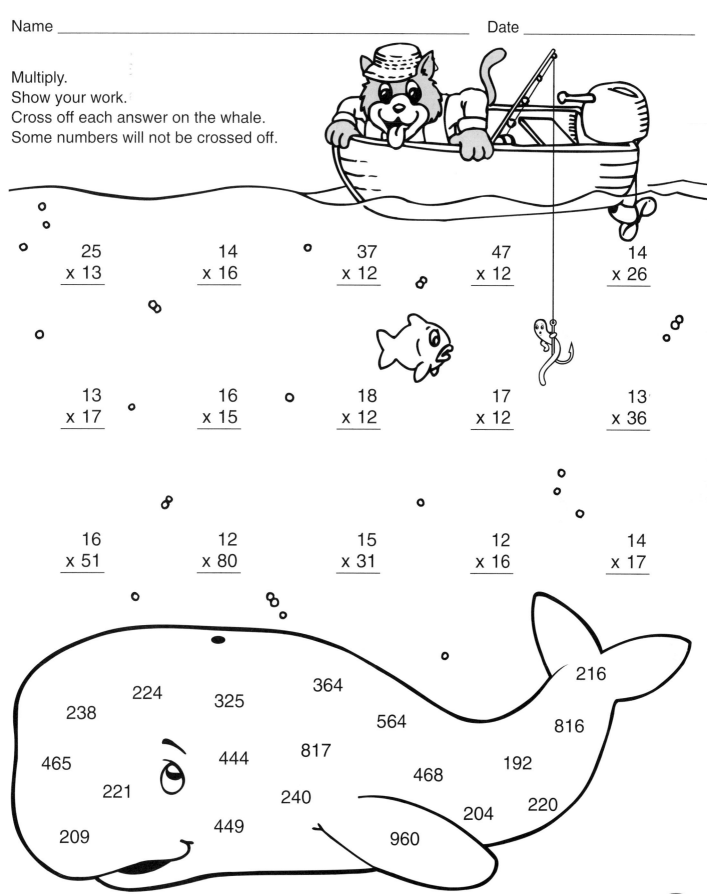

25	14	37	47	14
x 13	x 16	x 12	x 12	x 26

13	16	18	17	13
x 17	x 15	x 12	x 12	x 36

16	12	15	12	14
x 51	x 80	x 31	x 16	x 17

238   224   325   364   216

465   221   444   817   564   468   192   816

209   449   240   960   204   220

Counting Sheep

Name _____   Date _____

Multiply.
Show your work on another sheet of paper.
Color if correct.

26
x 13
___
339

35
x 12
___
427

18
x 14
___
252

45
x 12
___
540

27
x 13
___
351

28
x 13
___
364

17
x 14
___
238

48
x 12
___
576

12
x 17
___
209

29
x 13
___
377

19
x 14
___
266

46
x 20
___
926

15
x 14
___
219

15
x 16
___
240

2 digits x 2 digits with one regrouping

Cool Cats

Name _____ Date _____

Multiply.
Show your work.
To answer the riddle, write the matching letters on the numbered lines below.

45 x 12	24 x 13	49 x 12	17 x 15	16 x 13
= H	= V	= A	= O	= L

19 x 12	15 x 14	14 x 16	15 x 15	13 x 37
= T	= T	= R	= L	= Y

13 x 63	24 x 23	13 x 17	15 x 16	12 x 37
= O	= T	= A	= G	= I

What keeps jazz musicians on the earth?

___ ___ ___   ___ ___ ___ ___
588 208 225   210 540 221 228

" ___ ___ ___ ___ ___ ___ ___ ___ !"
  240 224 255 819 312 444 552 481

2 digits x 2 digits with one regrouping **57**

Mooseland Marvin

Name _____   Date _____

Read.
Solve each problem on another sheet of paper.
Write the answer in the blank.

WELCOME TO MOOSELAND PARK

1. Marvin's favorite snack is a willow twig. If he eats 16 twigs from 15 willow trees during the day, how many twigs will Marvin eat in all?

_____ twigs

2. Marvin crossed a stream 14 times today. If he crossed the stream this number of times each day for 17 days, how many times would Marvin cross the stream in all?

_____ times

3. Twelve tourist buses traveled through the park. Marvin nodded at them. If each bus carried 48 people, how many people were on the buses in all?

_____ people

4. Marvin made hoofprints in the mud. If he made 28 prints in one minute, how many hoofprints did he make in 13 minutes?

_____ hoofprints

5. Fourteen groups picnicked in the park. Each group had 25 people. If every person took a photo of Marvin, how many photos of Marvin were taken in all?

_____ photos

6. Marvin found 16 pieces of bubble gum in a bag. If he blew 13 bubbles with each piece of gum, how many bubbles did Marvin blow in all?

_____ bubbles

Sea of Stars

Multiply.
Show your work.
Color each starfish that has a matching answer.

218	291	108	121
x 14	x 21	x 17	x 38

145	181	109
x 12	x 41	x 71

113	262	141
x 37	x 13	x 27

140	371
x 72	x 12

8,938

6,111

1,836

4,181

7,421

1,740

8,080

3,807

4,598

4,452

3,406

3,052

4,498

10,080

1,121

7,739

Heading Home!

Name _____   Date _____

Multiply.
Show your work on another sheet of paper.
Cross off each answer on the rocket.
Some numbers will not be crossed off.

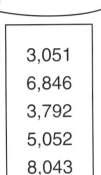

316 x 12	172 x 41	112 x 38
328 x 13	103 x 83	394 x 21
326 x 21	108 x 71	192 x 14
181 x 14	383 x 21	121 x 28
352 x 20	292 x 31	113 x 27

3,051
6,846
3,792
5,052
8,043
4,246
3,844
2,688
3,388
7,052
4,264
3,488
2,534
7,040
8,549
2,388
3,782
8,274
7,668
9,052
4,256

T-Bone's Top Trick

Name _____   Date _____

Multiply.
Show your work on another sheet of paper.
Color to show the path to the best trick.

Woofville Obedience School

Dog Tricks

112 x 82 =	9,184	9,634	9,284	9,084
328 x 31 =	10,028	10,168	9,968	10,348
140 x 25 =	3,500	3,550	3,300	3,390
151 x 12 =	1,782	1,812	1,912	1,712
364 x 20 =	6,280	8,180	7,280	7,260
127 x 13 =	1,540	1,731	1,642	1,651
242 x 24 =	5,728	5,708	5,808	6,258
231 x 14 =	3,134	3,324	3,234	3,243
218 x 41 =	8,848	8,638	8,738	8,938
241 x 32 =	7,812	7,912	7,712	7,412
462 x 21 =	9,302	9,702	10,602	8,702
232 x 42 =	10,644	9,734	9,744	8,944

rolling over	chasing his tail	catching a ball	fetching a stick

3 digits x 2 digits with one regrouping 61

Zoo Zaniness

Name _____   Date _____

Read.
Solve each problem on another sheet of paper.
Write the answer in the blank.

1. There are 12 tigers at the zoo learning how to box. If each tiger weighs 451 pounds, how many pounds do the tigers weigh in all?
   _____ pounds

Why should I flap faster?

2. One hummingbird's wings beat 192 times a minute. How many times will the bird's wings beat in 31 minutes?
   _____ times

3. The giant panda learning to ride a unicycle at the zoo eats 602 pounds of bamboo shoots each week. How many pounds of bamboo shoots will it eat in 13 weeks?
   _____ pounds

Hi! I'm Albert!

4. In one day, 141 people visited the smiling reptile exhibit. How many people will visit the exhibit in 52 days?
   _____ people

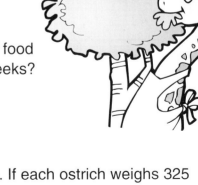

5. Each giraffe in the zoo's cooking school eats 490 pounds of food a week. How many pounds of food will a giraffe eat in 21 weeks?
   _____ pounds

OH, MY!

6. The zoo has 13 ostriches on diets. If each ostrich weighs 325 pounds, how many pounds do the ostriches weigh in all?
   _____ pounds

Story problems: 3 digits x 2 digits with one regrouping

Colossal Columns

Name _____ Date _____

Multiply.
Show your work.

2,123
x   14

1,214
x   42

2,402
x   13

1,083
x   31

2,126
x   31

3,006
x   21

3,152
x   12

1,502
x   14

2,540
x   12

©The Education Center, Inc. • *Target Math Success* • TEC60831 • Key p. 132

4 digits x 2 digits with one regrouping 63

Who Wins?

Name _____ Date _____

Multiply.
Show your work on another sheet of paper.
Color the boxes with the correct answers
  to show the path to the winner.

4,112 x 42 =	172,714	172,704	172,604	162,704
1,813 x 12 =	21,755	21,735	21,756	21,736
3,152 x 21 =	66,293	66,203	66,193	66,192
2,231 x 24 =	52,544	53,594	53,544	53,545
3,613 x 21 =	75,874	75,873	75,883	76,073
1,116 x 15 =	16,740	16,741	16,761	17,740
1,604 x 12 =	19,246	19,248	19,268	19,276
1,801 x 14 =	25,254	25,315	25,214	25,215
4,021 x 13 =	52,263	52,274	52,273	52,264
2,421 x 23 =	55,583	55,683	55,673	55,674
2,013 x 24 =	38,312	48,312	48,212	48,412
4,201 x 42 =	176,442	176,443	176,462	176,423

Barney

Boomer

Bailey

Buster

©The Education Center, Inc. • *Target Math Success* • TEC60831 • Key p. 132

64 **4 digits x 2 digits with one regrouping**

Keeping Things Spiffy!

Name _____ Date _____

Multiply.
Show your work.
Color each letter that has a matching answer.

1,113	2,061
x 16	x 31

4,202	3,010
x 14	x 72

2,004	1,108	5,011	1,008
x 41	x 16	x 12	x 19

What kind of fish cleans up after itself?

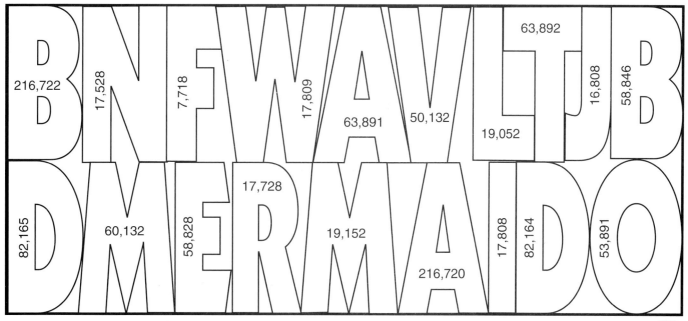

Taco Time!

Name _____ Date _____

Read.
Solve each problem on another sheet of paper.
Write the answer in the blank.

1. Paco has 12 big boxes of tacos. If each box holds 1,632 taco shells, how many shells does Paco have in all?

_____ shells

2. Paco has 15 different taco stands. If 1,102 tacos are sold at each stand, how many tacos will Paco sell in all?

_____ tacos

3. There are 14 large bags of shredded lettuce in Paco's refrigerator. If each bag contains 2,013 pieces of shredded lettuce, how many pieces does he have in all?

_____ pieces

4. Paco has 3,005 slices of cheese. If he shreds each slice into 13 pieces, how many cheese shreds will he have in all?

_____ shreds

5. There are 1,412 tomatoes being delivered to Paco's stand. If he cuts each tomato into 42 small cubes, how many cubes will he have in all?

_____ cubes

Paco's Taco Stand

Bull's-Eye!

Name ______________________________ Date ______________

Multiply.
Show your work.
Color by the code.

Code
odd = red
even = yellow

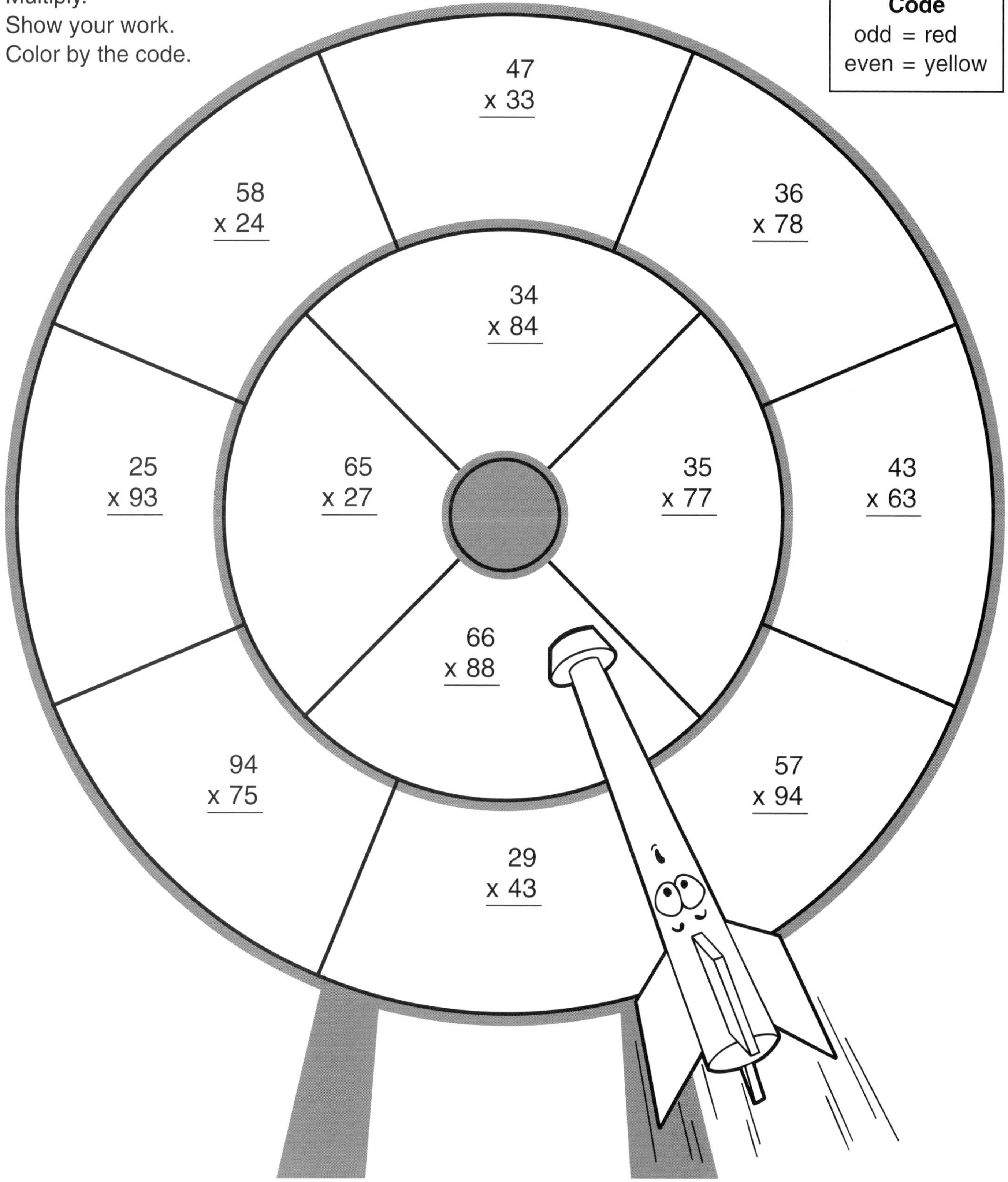

47 x 33
58 x 24
36 x 78
34 x 84
25 x 93
65 x 27
35 x 77
43 x 63
66 x 88
94 x 75
57 x 94
29 x 43

Nail It Down!

Name _____   Date _____

Multiply.
Show your work on another sheet of paper.
Write each letter in its matching blank below.

69
x 38
= N

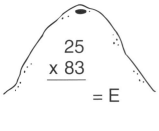
25
x 83
= E

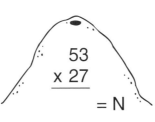
53
x 27
= N

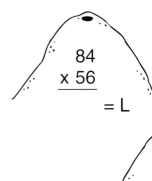
84
x 56
= L

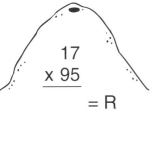
17
x 95
= R

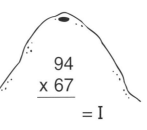
94
x 67
= I

72
x 28
= S

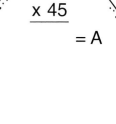
39
x 45
= A

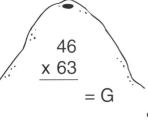
46
x 63
= G

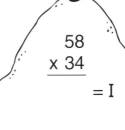
58
x 34
= I

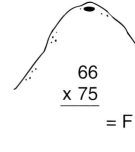
66
x 75
= F

What nails do carpenters hate to hit?

!

___ ___ ___ ___ ___ ___ ___ ___ ___ ___ ___
4,950 6,298 1,431 2,898 2,075 1,615 2,622 1,755 1,972 4,704 2,016

2 digits x 2 digits with one or more regroupings

Right at Home!

Name _____ Date _____

Multiply.
Show your work on another sheet of paper.
Color if correct.

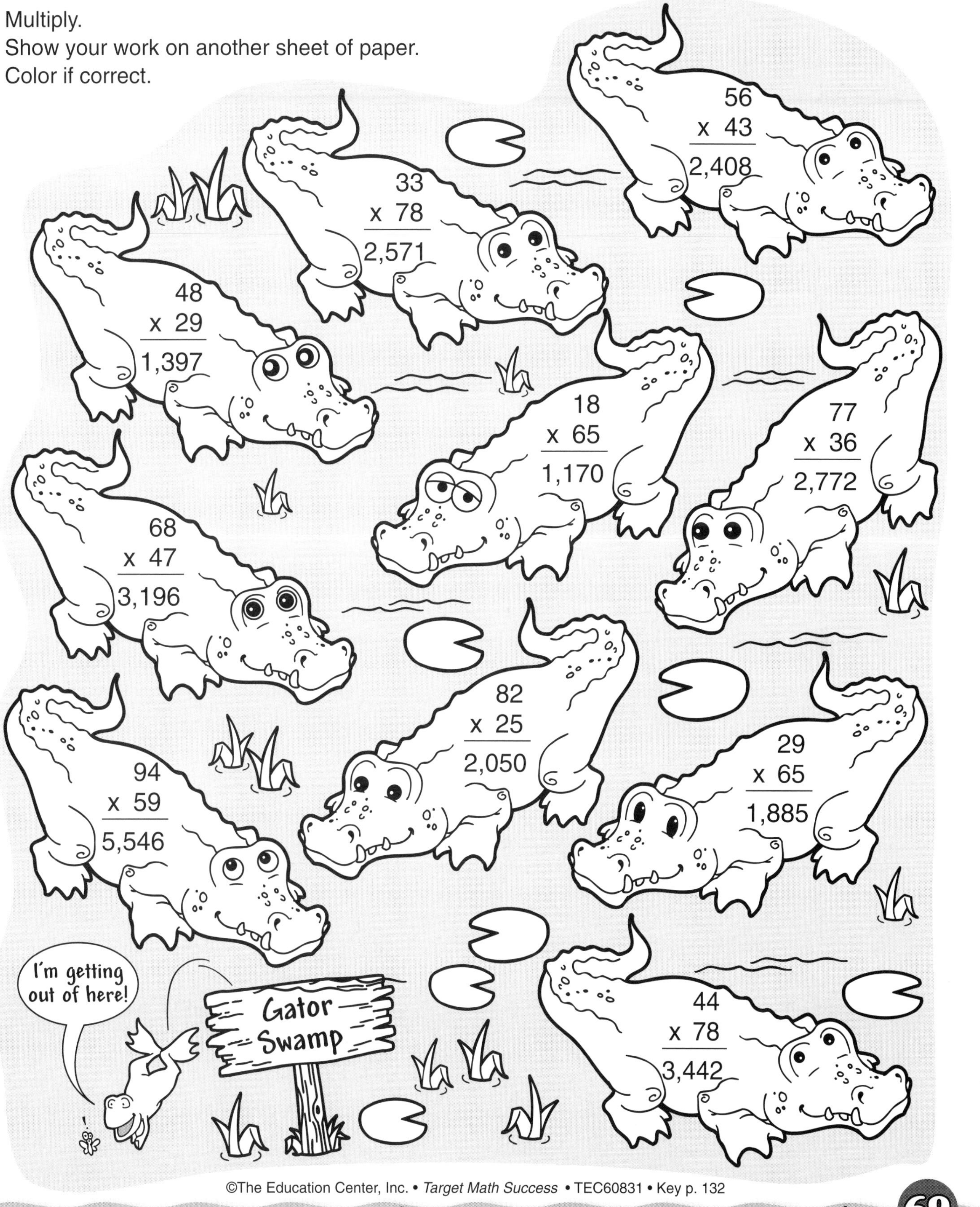

56
x 43
2,408

33
x 78
2,571

48
x 29
1,397

18
x 65
1,170

77
x 36
2,772

68
x 47
3,196

94
x 59
5,546

82
x 25
2,050

29
x 65
1,885

I'm getting
out of here!

Gator
Swamp

44
x 78
3,442

"Bone-a-fide" Doggie Treats

Name _____ Date _____

Read.
Solve each problem on another sheet of paper.
Write the answer in the blank.

1. Bowser's favorite doggie treats are on sale. Bowser buys 38 small boxes. If each box contains 26 treats, how many treats does he have in all?

_____ treats

2. Bowser's brother, Wowser, wants 32 large boxes of treats. If each large box contains 25 treats, how many treats will Wowser have in all?

_____ treats

3. The brothers want to try the new multiflavored treats. Together they buy 36 boxes. If each box contains 24 treats, how many treats do they have in all?

_____ treats

4. Their buddies buy 48 extra large boxes of treats. If each box contains 35 treats, how many treats do they have in all?

_____ treats

5. Bowser and Wowser buy 25 gift boxes of treats for their parents. If there are 15 treats in each box, how many treats do they buy in all?

_____ treats

6. The brothers buy 18 super-sized boxes for a party. If each box contains 52 treats, how many treats do they have in all?

_____ treats

Story problems: 2 digits x 2 digits with one or more regroupings

Let's Get Together!

Name _____ Date _____

Multiply.
Show your work.

We'd make a great pair!

287 x 33	394 x 52	456 x 39
165 x 84	506 x 88	637 x 92
714 x 63	820 x 46	959 x 73

Get a Strike!

Name _____   Date _____

Multiply.
Show your work.
To solve the riddle, write each letter in its matching blank.

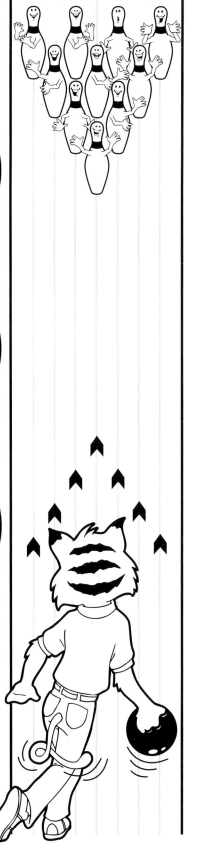

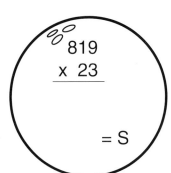

819
x 23

= S

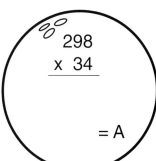

436
x 72

= E

298
x 34

= A

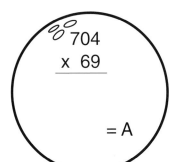

704
x 69

= A

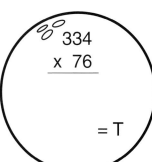

619
x 53

= L

334
x 76

= T

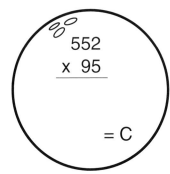

552
x 95

= C

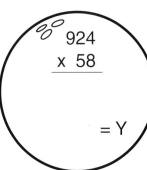

924
x 58

= Y

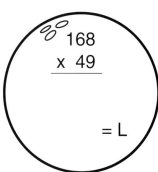

168
x 49

= L

What kind of cats go bowling?

___ ___ ___ ___ ___   ___ ___ ___ ___ !
48,576 8,232 32,807 31,392 53,592   52,440 10,132 25,384 18,837

3 digits x 2 digits with one or more regroupings

Bank It!

Name _____ Date _____

Multiply.
Show your work on another sheet of paper.
Color the coins that have correct answers.

614
x 85
52,190

242
x 97
23,474

336
x 54
18,144

178
x 63
11,201

821
x 49
40,229

592
x 36
21,318

915
x 77
70,455

132
x 59
7,788

484
x 24
11,616

Getting the Scoop on Ice Cream

Name _____ Date _____

Read.
Solve each problem on another sheet of paper.
Write the answer in the blank.

1. Today, 516 cartons of ice cream arrived at Super Scoops Ice-Cream Shoppe. If each carton contains 23 scoops of ice cream, how many scoops can be served in all?

   _____ scoops

2. Dippers Ice-Cream Company received a total of 842 orders for Choco-Berry ice cream. If the company gets that number of orders for 37 days, how many orders will it get in all?

   _____ orders

3. If an ice-cream delivery truck can hold 329 cartons of ice cream, how many cartons can 65 trucks hold in all?

   _____ cartons

4. Seventy-nine people scooped ice cream at Igloo Ice-Cream Store's grand opening. If each person made 284 scoops of ice cream, how many scoops were made in all?

   _____ scoops

5. Igloo Ice-Cream Store gave away 188 plastic ice-cream scoopers each hour during its grand opening. If the grand opening lasted 24 hours, how many plastic scoopers were given away in all?

   _____ plastic scoopers

6. Ida's Ice-Cream Shoppe gave away 782 free samples of ice cream today. If the shop gave away this number of samples each day for 48 days, how many samples would it give away in all?

   _____ samples

Safe and Sound

Name _____ Date _____

Multiply.
Show your work.
Write each answer in the magic square. The sum of each
    row and column should be 500,000.

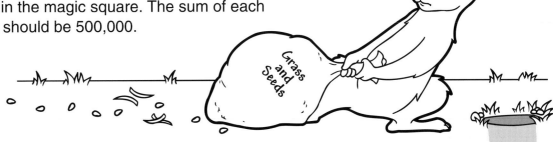

1.	1,253 x 42	2.	6,503 x 22	3.	8,453 x 36	4.	4,317 x 52

5.	5,640 x 44	6.	1,954 x 14	7.	7,190 x 31	8.	6,043 x 18

9.   7,014
    x   24

1.	2.	3.
4.	5.	6.
7.	8.	9.

Surrender?

Name _____ Date _____

Multiply.
Show your work on another sheet of paper.

Huh?

3,146	9,425	1,274	7,322
x 23	x 14	x 92	x 53

2,543	5,067	8,423	4,729
x 82	x 25	x 67	x 36

6,818	1,951	3,056	7,512
x 41	x 78	x 29	x 55

To find out what a white flag being waved in a car race means, color each space below that contains a correct answer.

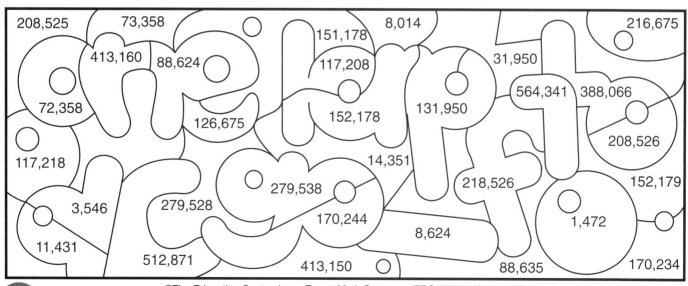

4 digits x 2 digits with one or more regroupings

Goal!

Multiply.
Show your work on another sheet of paper.
Color if correct.
Connect the colored soccer balls to show the
    path to the goal.

Start

2,669	6,314	4,871
x 28	x 35	x 51
74,632	220,990	248,421

8,125	9,073	3,286	2,743
x 43	x 61	x 48	x 27
349,470	553,453	155,728	74,050

5,902	7,497	1,528	3,084
x 73	x 54	x 94	x 85
430,364	404,838	140,632	262,130

5,532	1,627	2,950
x 37	x 66	x 77
204,684	107,182	227,157

6,733	9,251
x 38	x 33
255,854	305,283

Finish

Ants on Parade

Name _____ Date _____

Read.
Solve each problem on another sheet of paper.
Write the answer in the blank.

1. It took 4,069 ants to build the doughnut float.
   Each ant brought 75 flower petals for the float.
   How many flower petals did the ants bring
   in all?

   _____ flower petals

2. There were 47 floats in the parade. Only
   1,635 ants rode on each float. How many
   ants rode on floats in all?

   _____ ants

3. There were 1,574 ants throwing candy crumbs.
   Each ant threw 58 candy crumbs. How many crumbs
   did the ants throw in all?

   _____ crumbs

4. It took 26 ants to hold the great ant balloon during the
   parade. Each of the ants walked 2,548 steps. How many
   steps did the ants take in all?

   _____ steps

5. Every band in the parade had 3,915 instruments. If 38 bands
   marched in the parade, how many instruments were there in all?

   _____ instruments

6. There were 72 cleanup crews. Each crew had 6,022 ants.
   How many ants cleaned up after the parade?

   _____ ants

Story problems: 4 digits x 2 digits with one or more regroupings

What's Cooking?

Multiply.
Cross off each answer on the spoon.
Some numbers will not be crossed off.

324 x 192	898 x 207	462 x 116
528 x 633	275 x 319	924 x 786
653 x 218	885 x 671	759 x 596	463 x 781

726,264

185,836

593,835

334,224

87,705

142,354

185,886

53,592

87,725

452,364

361,603

62,208

142,334

3 digits x 3 digits with one or more regroupings 79

Whale Watch

Name _____   Date _____

Multiply.
Show your work on another sheet of paper.
Color to show the path to the whale.

What kind of whale is that?

264 x 319 =	74,216	84,186	84,216	83,216
583 x 748 =	436,064	436,084	435,084	436,184
126 x 482 =	60,732	55,932	60,722	58,732
855 x 671 =	573,605	573,705	569,705	573,305
967 x 223 =	215,632	215,621	215,641	214,641
435 x 309 =	133,415	134,515	134,375	134,415
617 x 761 =	465,537	469,137	468,637	469,537
592 x 816 =	481,072	483,062	483,072	473,072
148 x 994 =	135,124	147,112	146,412	147,012
356 x 872 =	310,432	310,332	310,341	306,932
471 x 289 =	136,119	136,109	135,519	136,019
628 x 570 =	353,960	357,960	347,960	357,460

killer whale

humpback whale

gray whale

blue whale

Baby's First Picture

Name _____   Date _____

Multiply.
Show your work.

Smile!

1,483 x 715	2,714 x 326

5,062 x 239	3,918 x 454	1,635 x 182

6,401 x 395	2,341 x 513

4 digits x 3 digits with one or more regroupings   **83**

Bunches of Butterflies

Name _____ Date _____

Multiply.
Show your work on another sheet of paper.
Color by the code.

(p) 1,270 x 342 = _____

(r) 4,516 x 278 = _____

(g) 7,383 x 502 = _____

(o) 5,421 x 147 = _____

(r) 3,167 x 435 = _____

(y) 2,742 x 916 = _____

(b) 1,095 x 823 = _____

(r) 2,938 x 634 = _____

(g) 6,154 x 750 = _____

(o) 3,529 x 562 = _____

(g) 4,613 x 138 = _____

(p) 8,251 x 249 = _____

796,887

901,185

1,983,298

636,594

3,706,266

1,377,645

1,255,448

2,511,672

2,054,499

434,340

4,615,500

1,862,692

Color Code
b = blue   y = yellow
o = orange g = green
p = purple r = red

4 digits x 3 digits with one or more regroupings

Open Wide!

Name _____   Date _____

Multiply.
Show your work.
To solve the riddle, match the letters to
    the numbered lines below.

```
  2,506              3,627
x   621            x   225
```

= I   = N

```
  8,172      4,324          1,905          5,268
x   152    x   348        x   517        x   118
```

= L   = A   = !   = G

```
  2,433      4,151          1,573
x   460    x   309        x   296
```

= I   = L   = F

Why did the pie crust go to the dentist?

It needed _____ _____ _____ _____ _____ _____ _____ _____
         1,504,752   465,608 1,556,226 1,282,659 1,242,144 1,119,180   816,075   621,624   984,885

Opal's Orchard

Name _____ Date _____

Read.
Solve each problem on another sheet of paper.
Write the answer in the blank.

1. There are 1,425 apple trees in Opal's orchard. Each tree has 215 apples. How many apples are there in all?

   _____ apples

2. After sorting out the wormy apples, Opal has 2,067 bushels of apples. There are 144 apples in each bushel. How many wormless apples does Opal have?

   _____ wormless apples

3. Opal has 2,909 pounds of wormy apples. There are 113 worms in each pound. How many worms are there in all?

   _____ worms

4. Opal uses ladybugs for pest control. She bought 368 cartons of ladybugs. Each carton has 1,538 ladybugs inside. How many ladybugs are there in all?

   _____ ladybugs

5. If Opal's orchard needs 7,515 gallons of water a day, how many gallons will it need for 189 days?

   _____ gallons of water

6. Opal plants 1,594 rows of apple seeds. She puts 572 seeds in each row. How many apple seeds does she plant in all?

   _____ apple seeds

Story problems: 4 digits x 3 digits with one or more regroupings

Properties and Strategies

Properties and Strategies

Table of Contents

Outer Space or Bust!

Name _____ Date _____

Color each star that shows the commutative property.

93 x 12 = 1,116
18 x 62 = 1,116

610 x 7 = 4,270
7 x 610 = 4,270

75 x 6 = 450
6 x 75 = 450

28 x 11 = 308
11 x 28 = 308

Finish

23 x 41 = 943
40 x 23 = 920

8 x 7 = 56
4 x 14 = 56

33 x 5 = 165
5 x 33 = 165

120 x 50 = 6,000
600 x 10 = 6,000

9 x 8 = 72
8 x 19 = 152

16 x 24 = 384
32 x 12 = 384

47 x 12 = 564
12 x 47 = 564

17 x 21 = 357
21 x 17 = 357

25 x 103 = 2,575
103 x 25 = 2,575

50 x 4 = 200
4 x 25 = 100

56 x 14 = 784
16 x 49 = 784

18 x 3 = 54
9 x 6 = 54

90 x 2 = 180
3 x 60 = 180

13 x 3 = 39
3 x 13 = 39

45 x 3 = 135
46 x 3 = 138

Start

7 x 25 = 175
25 x 7 = 175

9 x 7 = 63
7 x 9 = 63

8 x 6 = 48
6 x 7 = 42

Commutative property 89

Crocs Rock!

Name _____ Date _____

Multiply.
Show your work on another sheet of paper.
On each rock, write a new multiplication sentence that shows the commutative property.

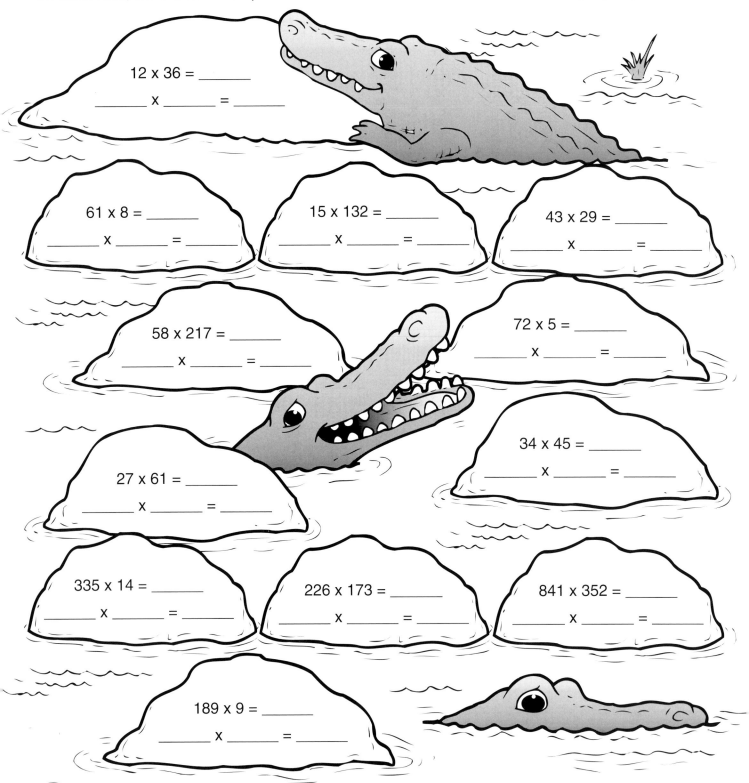

12 x 36 = _____
_____ x _____ = _____

61 x 8 = _____
_____ x _____ = _____

15 x 132 = _____
_____ x _____ = _____

43 x 29 = _____
_____ x _____ = _____

58 x 217 = _____
_____ x _____ = _____

72 x 5 = _____
_____ x _____ = _____

34 x 45 = _____
_____ x _____ = _____

27 x 61 = _____
_____ x _____ = _____

335 x 14 = _____
_____ x _____ = _____

226 x 173 = _____
_____ x _____ = _____

841 x 352 = _____
_____ x _____ = _____

189 x 9 = _____
_____ x _____ = _____

Snacktime!

Name _____ Date _____

Multiply.
Show your work on another sheet of paper.
Color each box that shows an example of the associative property.
Connect the colored boxes to show a path to the peanuts.

(22 x 4) x 167 =
22 x (4 x 167) =

63 x (5 x 1,126) =
(5 x 63) x 1,126 =

5 x (16 x 1,974) =
(5 x 16) x 1,972 =

(774 x 21) x 3 =
774 x (21 x 3) =

1 x (52 x 63) =
(1 x 52) x 63 =

(863 x 4) x 24 =
(24 x 4) x 863 =

95 x (8 x 112) =
(95 x 8) x 112 =

(46 x 33) x 1,104 =
46 x (33 x 1,104) =

(266 x 12) x 5 =
266 x (3 x 20) =

62 x (11 x 526) =
(62 x 11) x 526 =

(86 x 8) x 350 =
86 x (350 x 8) =

29 x (14 x 174) =
(29 x 14) x 174 =

3 x (18 x 56) =
(2 x 27) x 56 =

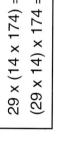

PEANUTS

(91 x 16) x 825 =
91 x (825 x 16) =

(111 x 68) x 7 =
111 x (68 x 7) =

53 x (8 x 1,272) =
(53 x 8) x 1,272 =

(724 x 4) x 12 =
724 x (4 x 12) =

Night-Light Support

Name _____   Date _____

Multiply.
Write a new multiplication sentence to show the associative property.
To solve the riddle, match the letters to the numbered lines below.

36 x (5 x 503) = _____

___ x ___ x ___ = _____
        S

(8 x 1,096) x 13 = _____

___ x ___ x ___ = _____

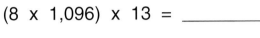

(805 x 7) x 4 = _____

___ x ___ x ___ = _____
        M

52 x (86 x 64) = _____

___ x ___ x ___ = _____
        T

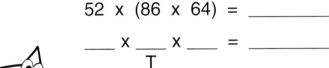

4,643 x (5 x 32) = _____

___ x ___ x ___ = _____
A

(27 x 3) x 226 = _____

___ x ___ x ___ = _____
        E

(9 x 4) x 721 = _____

___ x ___ x ___ = _____

17 x (6 x 5,196) = _____

___ x ___ x ___ = _____
      S

(9 x 901) x 26 = _____

___ x ___ x ___ = _____
        B

(73 x 362) x 2 = _____

___ x ___ x ___ = _____
I

What keeps the moon from falling?

_____ _____ _____   _____ _____ _____ _____
  73   86   17   210,834   226   4,643   22,540   503

Quick Quilt

Name _____ Date _____

Multiply.
Show your work on another sheet of paper.
Color by the code.

Color Code
Commutative property = pink
Zero property = blue
Property of one = orange
Associative property = yellow

87 x 3 = _____ 3 x 87 = _____	46 x 0 = _____	719 x 0 = _____	15 x 9 = _____ 9 x 15 = _____
329 x 5 = _____ 5 x 329 = _____	64 x 1 = _____	28 x 1 = _____	433 x 12 = _____ 12 x 433 = _____
26 x 0 = _____	14 x (5 x 21) = _____	(37 x 80) x 19 = _____	3,431 x 0 = _____
347 x 1 = _____	(14 x 5) x 21 = _____	37 x (80 x 19) = _____	1,468 x 1 = _____
51 x 1 = _____	(702 x 3) x 64 = _____	1,208 x (2 x 316) = _____	236 x 1 = _____
93 x 0 = _____	702 x (3 x 64) = _____	(1,208 x 2) x 316 = _____	14 x 0 = _____
128 x 14 = _____ 14 x 128 = _____	7,091 x 1 = _____	18 x 1 = _____	72 x 56 = _____ 56 x 72 = _____
31 x 518 = _____ 518 x 31 = _____	535 x 0 = _____	6,079 x 0 = _____	63 x 7 = _____ 7 x 63 = _____

Which Way Down?

Name _____ Date _____

Multiply.
Show your work on another sheet of paper.
To show the path down the tree, color the box of the property shown.

913 x 7 = 7 x 913 = _____

(26 x 3) x 14 = 26 x (3 x 14) = _____

16 x 25 = 25 x 16 = _____

503 x 1 = _____

316 x 0 = _____

6,718 x 1 = _____

1,312 x 247 = 247 x 1,312 = _____

(317 x 2) x 51 = 317 x (2 x 51) = _____

46 x (13 x 245) = (46 x 13) x 245 = _____

22 x 6,051 = 6,051 x 22 = _____

49 x 2,016 = 2,016 x 49 = _____

9,087 x 1 = _____

Commutative Property	Property of One	Zero Property	Associative Property
Property of One	Associative Property	Zero Property	Commutative Property
Property of One	Associative Property	Commutative Property	Zero Property
Associative Property	Commutative Property	Property of One	Zero Property
Property of One	Associative Property	Commutative Property	Zero Property
Commutative Property	Zero Property	Associative Property	Property of One
Zero Property	Property of One	Commutative Property	Associative Property
Property of One	Associative Property	Commutative Property	Zero Property
Commutative Property	Zero Property	Associative Property	Property of One
Property of One	Zero Property	Associative Property	Commutative Property
Zero Property	Property of One	Commutative Property	Associative Property
Associative Property	Property of One	Zero Property	Commutative Property

properties of multiplication

Climbing Koala

Name _____   Date _____

Round to the greatest place value and multiply.
The first problem has been done for you.
Color by the code.

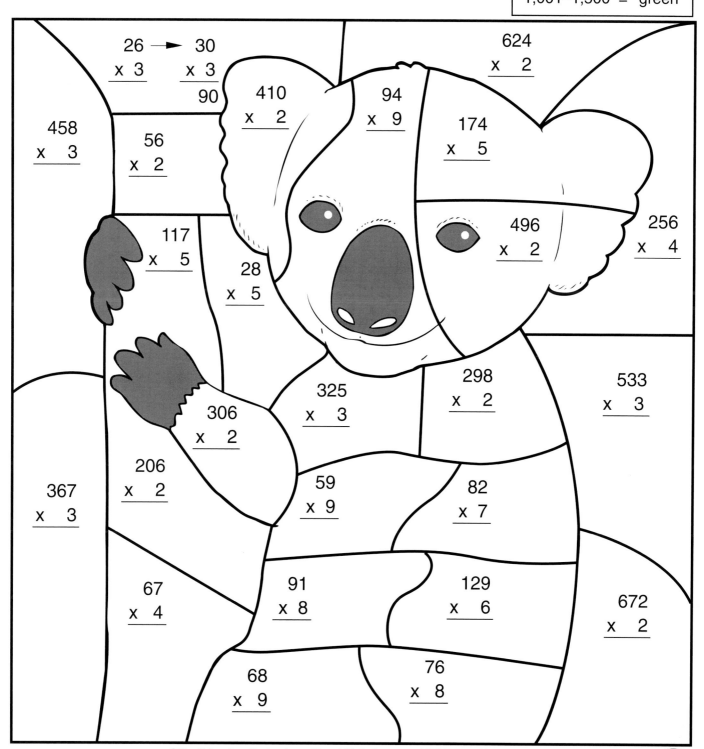

26 → 30
x 3   x 3
        90

624
x 2

458
x 3

56
x 2

410
x 2

94
x 9

174
x 5

117
x 5

28
x 5

496
x 2

256
x 4

306
x 2

325
x 3

298
x 2

533
x 3

206
x 2

59
x 9

82
x 7

367
x 3

67
x 4

91
x 8

129
x 6

672
x 2

68
x 9

76
x 8

Toad on the Road

Name _____   Date _____

Round to the greatest place value and multiply.
Show your work on another sheet of paper.
The first two problems have been done for you.
To solve the riddle, match the letters to the
   numbered lines below.

A. 256 x 53   300 x 50 = 15,000

G. 91 x 3   90 x 3 = 270   H. 872 x 2

F. 5,097 x 7   S. 32 x 26

O. 1,726 x 42   E. 754 x 12

C. 72 x 86   G. 690 x 6

T. 38 x 9   R. 899 x 31

R. 429 x 76   T. 974 x 11

O. 36 x 7   A. 6,504 x 27

D. 567 x 4   O. 49 x 22

              T. 76 x 7

What happened when the frog parked its car in a no parking zone?

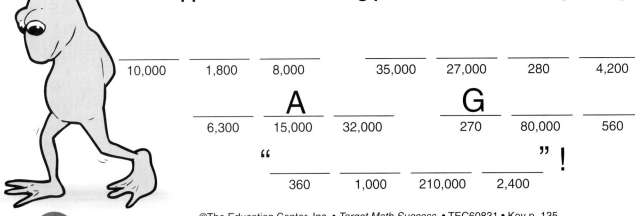

_____ _____ _____   _____ _____ _____ _____ _____ ,
10,000 1,800 8,000   35,000 27,000 280 4,200 900

_____ A _____   G _____ _____
6,300 15,000 32,000   270 80,000 560

" _____ _____ _____ _____ " !
  360 1,000 210,000 2,400

Curling Up With a Good Book

Name _____ Date _____

Read.
Round to the greatest place value. Estimate an answer for each problem.
Write your estimate in the blank.

1. The bookstore Curl Up With a Good Book has 187 bookcases. Each bookcase holds 328 books. About how many books are there in all?

    _____ books

2. Twenty-nine customers are buying children's books. If each customer buys 4 books, about how many children's books will be sold in all?

    _____ children's books

3. The bookstore sells 499 magazines each month. If the same amount is sold each month for 9 months, about how many magazines will be sold in all?

    _____ magazines

4. Seven people work at the bookstore. If each worker sells 296 books this week, about how many books will be sold in all?

    _____ books

5. The bookstore receives 2,004 new books each month. If the same amount is received each month for 12 months, about how many books will be received in all?

    _____ books

6. Twenty-seven famous authors visit the bookstore each year. If each author signs 3,342 books, about how many books will be signed in all?

    _____ books

7. Each day the customers in the bookstore read a total of 6,008 pages. If the same amount of pages is read for 206 days, about how many pages will be read in all?

    _____ pages

8. Each month, the bookstore sells 615 newspapers. If the same amount is sold each month for 19 months, about how many newspapers will be sold in all?

    _____ newspapers

Afternoon Snooze Tune

Name _____ Date _____

Color the notes that are multiples of 10.

20

9,000

8,100

10,200

1,600

100,100

801

1,000,000

780

30,000

15,000

408

906

56

890

505

201

100

Al's Abstract Art

Name _____ Date _____

Multiply.
Show your work on another sheet of paper.
Color by the code.

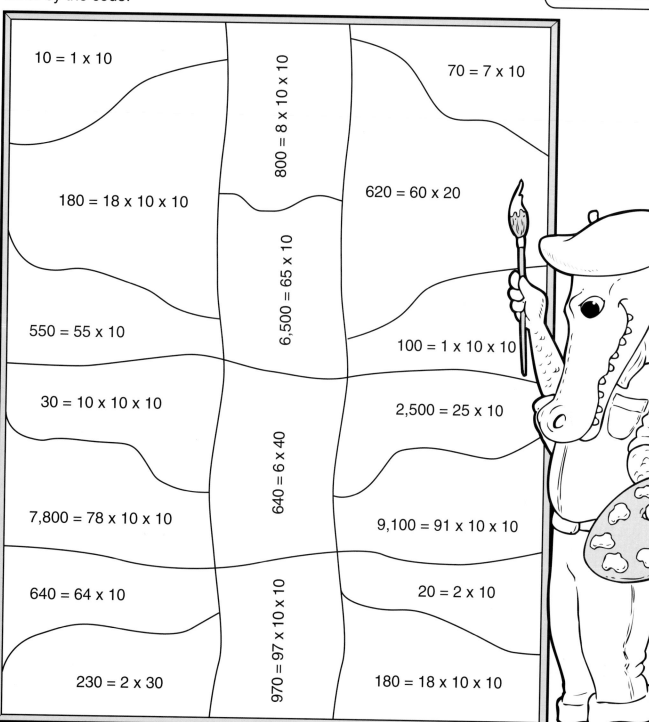

10 = 1 x 10

800 = 8 x 10 x 10

70 = 7 x 10

180 = 18 x 10 x 10

620 = 60 x 20

6,500 = 65 x 10

550 = 55 x 10

100 = 1 x 10 x 10

30 = 10 x 10 x 10

2,500 = 25 x 10

640 = 6 x 40

7,800 = 78 x 10 x 10

9,100 = 91 x 10 x 10

640 = 64 x 10

970 = 97 x 10 x 10

20 = 2 x 10

230 = 2 x 30

180 = 18 x 10 x 10

Sandwich and Bag Matchup

Name _____   Date _____

Multiply.
Show your work on another sheet of paper.
Write the answer in the blank.
Color by the code.

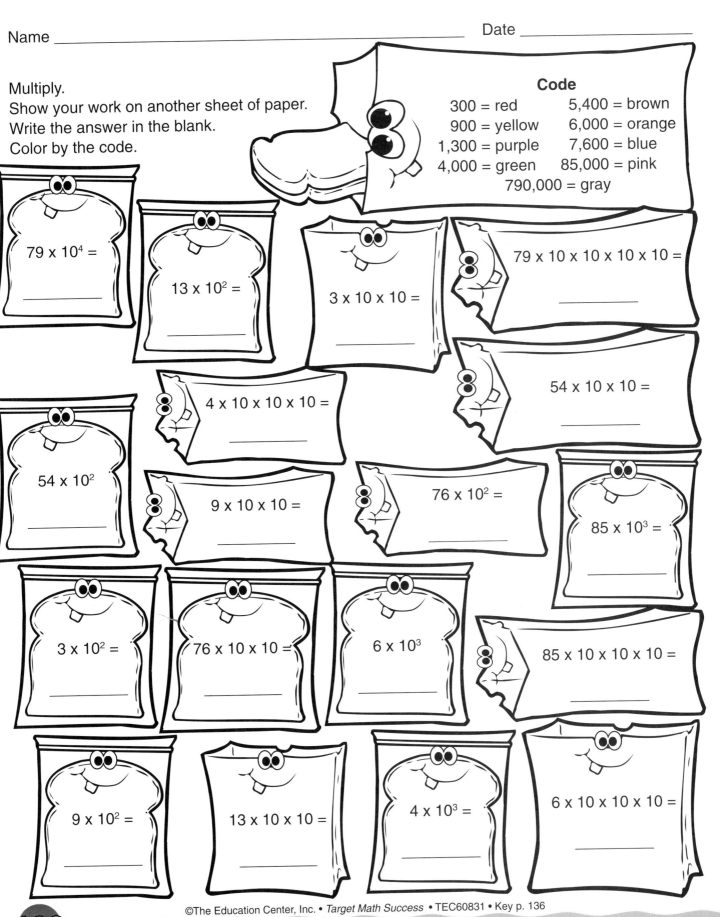

Code

300 = red	5,400 = brown
900 = yellow	6,000 = orange
1,300 = purple	7,600 = blue
4,000 = green	85,000 = pink
790,000 = gray	

79×10^4 =

13×10^2 =

$3 \times 10 \times 10$ =

$79 \times 10 \times 10 \times 10 \times 10$ = _____

$54 \times 10 \times 10$ =

$4 \times 10 \times 10 \times 10$ = _____

54×10^2

$9 \times 10 \times 10$ = _____

76×10^2 =

85×10^3 =

3×10^2 =

$76 \times 10 \times 10$ =

6×10^3

$85 \times 10 \times 10 \times 10$ =

9×10^2 =

$13 \times 10 \times 10$ =

4×10^3 =

$6 \times 10 \times 10 \times 10$ = _____

Parent Communication and Student Checkups

Parent Communication and Student Checkups

Table of Contents

How to Administer the Checkups

Both checkups can be given at the same time, or Checkup B can be given as a follow-up test for students who did not do well on Checkup A. The checkups will help you determine which students have mastered a skill and which students may need more practice.

Show-Your-Work Grids

For students who need help aligning numbers properly when writing vertical multiplication problems, check out the show-your-work grids on pages 120–121.

Student Progress Chart

(student)		Date	Number Correct	Comments
Checkup 1: Multiplying 2 digits x 1 digit without regrouping	A			
	B			
Checkup 2: Multiplying 3 digits x 1 digit with one regrouping	A			
	B			
Checkup 3: Multiplying 4 digits x 1 digit with one or more regroupings	A			
	B			
Checkup 4: Multiplying 2 digits x 2 digits without regrouping	A			
	B			
Checkup 5: Multiplying 3 digits x 2 digits with one regrouping	A			
	B			
Checkup 6: Multiplying 4 digits x 2 digits with one or more regroupings	A			
	B			
Checkup 7: Multiplying 3 digits x 3 digits with one or more regroupings	A			
	B			
Checkup 8: Multiplying 4 digits x 3 digits with one or more regroupings	A			
	B			

It's Time to Take Aim!

On _____ our class will be having a checkup on multiplication of larger numbers. To help your child prepare, please spend about 20 minutes reviewing math problems that involve **multiplying a two-digit number by a one-digit number without regrouping.** Thanks for your help!

Target These!

1.   23
    x 3

2.   14
    x 2

3.   12
    x 4

4.   11
    x 9

5.   32
    x 3

6.   42
    x 2

7.   20
    x 3

8.   21
    x 4

Try using these two steps!

Multiplication Refresher

Need help explaining to your child how to multiply a two-digit number by a one-digit number without regrouping? Try using the two-step method below. Walk your child through the first problem at the right using this method. Next, have him complete the second problem on his own, verbalizing each step as he solves the problem. Then have him complete the remaining problems independently.

Step 1
Multiply the ones.

T	O
2	3
X	3
	9

Step 2
Multiply the tens.

T	O
2	3
X	3
6	9

Answers: 69; 28; 48; 99; 96; 84; 60; 84

If your child is quick to solve the remaining math problems correctly, an occasional review may be all he or she needs. But if several of the answers are incorrect, it's a good idea to spend some time each day having your child work through a problem or two at home until he or she has mastered this skill.

Checkup 1

Name _____

Date _____

A.	32 x 3	11 x 8	12 x 2	21 x 4	22 x 3
B.	14 x 2	42 x 2	12 x 3	20 x 4	11 x 5
C.	44 x 2	33 x 3	21 x 2	34 x 2	11 x 3
D.	11 x 7	30 x 2	20 x 3	24 x 2	23 x 3

Checkup 1

Name _____

Date _____

A.	23 x 2	30 x 3	33 x 2	43 x 2	22 x 4
B.	11 x 6	12 x 4	31 x 3	40 x 2	22 x 2
C.	30 x 3	32 x 2	11 x 9	41 x 2	21 x 3
D.	13 x 2	31 x 2	13 x 3	14 x 2	11 x 4

It's Time to Take Aim!

On _____ our class will be having a checkup on multiplication of larger numbers. To help your child prepare, please spend about 20 minutes reviewing math problems that involve **multiplying a three-digit number by a one-digit number with one regrouping.** Thanks for your help!

Multiplication Refresher

Need help explaining to your child how to multiply a three-digit number by a one-digit number with one regrouping? Try using the three-step method below. Walk your child through the first problem at the right using this method. Next, have her complete the second problem on her own, verbalizing each step as she solves the problem. Then have her complete the remaining problems independently.

Step 1
Multiply the ones. Regroup if necessary.

H	T	O
	1	
1	3	7
X		2
		4

Regroup.

Step 2
Multiply the tens.
Add any regrouped tens.
Regroup if necessary.

H	T	O
	1	
1	3	7
X		2
	7	4

Step 3
Multiply the hundreds.
Add any regrouped hundreds.
(This problem has no regrouped hundreds.)
Regroup if necessary.

H	T	O
	1	
1	3	7
X		2
2	7	4

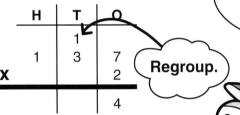

Try using these three steps!

Target These!

1.
```
  137
x   2
```

2.
```
  226
x   3
```

3.
```
  121
x   7
```

4.
```
  107
x   9
```

5.
```
  121
x   6
```

6.
```
  231
x   4
```

7.
```
  150
x   5
```

8.
```
  183
x   2
```

Answers: 274; 678; 847; 963; 726; 924; 750; 366

If your child is quick to solve the remaining math problems correctly, an occasional review may be all he or she needs. But if several of the answers are incorrect, it's a good idea to spend some time each day having your child work through a problem or two at home until he or she has mastered this skill.

Checkup 2

Name _____

Date _____

A. 316   142   237
    x 3   x 4   x 2

B. 463   219   407
    x 2   x 3   x 2

C. 153   231   304
    x 2   x 4   x 3

Test A: 3 digits x 1 digit with one regrouping

©The Education Center, Inc. • *Target Math Success* • TEC60831 • Key p. 136

Checkup 2

Name _____

Date _____

A. 405   152   361
    x 2   x 4   x 3

B. 227   482   393
    x 3   x 2   x 2

C. 374   208   192
    x 2   x 4   x 2

Test B: 3 digits x 1 digit with one regrouping

©The Education Center, Inc. • *Target Math Success* • TEC60831 • Key p. 136

It's Time to Take Aim!

On _____ our class will be having a checkup on multiplication of larger numbers. To help your child prepare, please spend about 20 minutes reviewing math problems that involve **multiplying a four-digit number by a one-digit number with one or more regroupings.** Thanks for your help!

Multiplication Refresher

Need help explaining to your child how to multiply a four-digit number by a one-digit number with one or more regroupings? Try using the four-step method below. Walk your child through the first problem at the right using this method. Next, have him complete the second problem on his own, verbalizing each step as he solves the problem. Then have him complete the remaining problems independently.

Step 1
Multiply the ones. Regroup if necessary.

Th	H	T	O
1	8	¹3	9
X			2
			8

Regroup.

Step 2
Multiply the tens.
Add any regrouped tens. Regroup if necessary.

Th	H	T	O
1	8	¹3	9
X			2
		7	8

Steps 3 and 4
Continue in the manner described for the remaining two digits.

Th	H	T	O
¹1	8	¹3	9
X			2
3,	6	7	8

Try using these four steps!

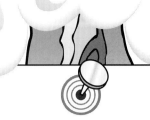

Target These!

1. 1,839
   x   2

2. 5,462
   x   6

3. 9,217
   x   5

4. 4,763
   x   2

5. 2,334
   x   3

6. 6,817
   x   4

7. 7,249
   x   9

8. 1,924
   x   7

Answers: 3,678; 32,772; 46,085; 9,526; 7,002; 27,268; 65,241; 13,468

©The Education Center, Inc. • *Target Math Success* • TEC60831

Checkup 3

Name _____   Date _____

A.   4,123
     x   4

     6,612
     x   5

     8,471
     x   7

B.   9,453
     x   3

     7,682
     x   8

     1,816
     x   2

C.   3,562
     x   6

     2,096
     x   9

     5,527
     x   3

D.   7,814
     x   5

     3,181
     x   8

     9,983
     x   4

Test A: 4 digits x 1 digit with one or more regroupings

Checkup 3

Name _____   Date _____

A.   3,948
     x   5

     1,776
     x   6

     8,457
     x   2

B.   5,073
     x   8

     4,684
     x   3

     6,539
     x   6

C.   9,198
     x   4

     7,347
     x   9

     2,780
     x   7

D.   5,645
     x   3

     8,298
     x   5

     4,028
     x   9

Test B: 4 digits x 1 digit with one or more regroupings

It's Time to Take Aim!

On _____ our class will be having a checkup on multiplication of larger numbers. To help your child prepare, please spend about 20 minutes reviewing math problems that involve **multiplying a two-digit number by a two-digit number without regrouping.** Thanks for your help!

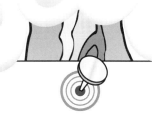

Target These!

1.	23 x 12	2.	14 x 12
3.	13 x 22	4.	45 x 11
5.	24 x 21	6.	33 x 22
7.			11 x 16
8.			31 x 23

Multiplication Refresher

Need help explaining to your child how to multiply a two-digit number by a two-digit number without regrouping? Try using the three-step method below. Walk your child through the first problem at the right using this method. Next, have her complete the second problem on her own, verbalizing each step as she solves the problem. Then have her complete the remaining problems independently.

Step 1
Multiply by the ones.

	H	T	O
		2	3
X		1	**2**
		4	6

Step 2
Write a zero to hold the ones place. Multiply by the tens.

	H	T	O
		2	3
X		1	2
		4	6
	2	3	**0**

Step 3
Add.

	H	T	O
		2	3
X		1	2
		4	6
+	2	3	0
	2	7	6

> Try using these three steps!

If your child is quick to solve the remaining math problems correctly, an occasional review may be all he or she needs. But if several of the answers are incorrect, it's a good idea to spend some time each day having your child work through a problem or two at home until he or she has mastered this skill.

Checkup 4

Name _____ Date _____

A.   42   21   12
    x 12   x 34   x 23

B.   35   22   23
    x 11   x 13   x 21

C.   43   18   33
    x 22   x 11   x 23

Test A: 2 digits x 2 digits without regrouping

©The Education Center, Inc. • *Target Math Success* • TEC60831 • Key p. 136

Checkup 4

Name _____ Date _____

A.   31   24   29
    x 22   x 12   x 11

B.   33   43   22
    x 12   x 21   x 23

C.   67   21   43
    x 11   x 14   x 12

Test B: 2 digits x 2 digits without regrouping

©The Education Center, Inc. • *Target Math Success* • TEC60831 • Key p. 136

It's Time to Take Aim!

On _____ our class will be having a checkup on multiplication of larger numbers. To help your child prepare, please spend about 20 minutes reviewing math problems that involve **multiplying a three-digit number by a two-digit number with one regrouping.** Thanks for your help!

Multiplication Refresher

Need help explaining to your child how to multiply a three-digit number by a two-digit number with one regrouping? Try using the three-step method below. Walk your child through the first problem at the right using this method. Next, have him complete the second problem on his own, verbalizing each step as he solves the problem. Then have him complete the remaining problems independently.

Step 1
Multiply by the ones.
Regroup if necessary.

H	T	O
4	6	1
X	2	1
4	6	1

Step 2
Write a zero to hold the ones place.
Multiply by the tens. Regroup if necessary.

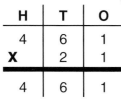

¹4	6	1
X	2	1
	4	6	1
9	2	2	0

Regroup.

Step 3
Add.

	H	T	O
	¹4	6	1
X		2	1
	4	6	1
+ 9	2	2	0
9,	6	8	1

Try using these three steps!

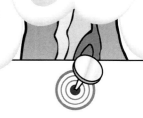

Practice These!

1. 461
    x 21

2. 291
    x 31

3. 204
    x 23

4. 119
    x 21

5. 145
    x 12

6. 113
    x 37

7. 151
    x 41

8. 140
    x 72

Answers: 9,681; 9,021; 4,692; 2,499; 1,740; 4,181; 6,191; 10,080

Checkup 5

Name _____

Date _____

A.
```
  272        180        453
x  31      x  31      x  21
```

B.
```
  213        162        491
x  14      x  41      x  12
```

C.
```
  394        192        417
x  21      x  30      x  21
```

Test A: 3 digits x 2 digits with one regrouping

©The Education Center, Inc. • Target Math Success • TEC60831 • Key p. 136

Checkup 5

Name _____

Date _____

A.
```
  254        352        471
x  12      x  31      x  40
```

B.
```
  281        415        227        108
x  13      x  20      x  21      x  14
```

C.
```
  164        309        217        184
x  12      x  31      x  41      x  21
```

Test B: 3 digits x 2 digits with one regrouping

©The Education Center, Inc. • Target Math Success • TEC60831 • Key p. 136

It's Time to Take Aim!

On _____ our class will be having a checkup on multiplication of larger numbers. To help your child prepare, please spend about 20 minutes reviewing math problems that involve **multiplying a four-digit number by a two-digit number with one or more regroupings.** Thanks for your help!

Target These!

1.	1,152	2.	1,462
	x 43		x 34

3. 4,167
    x   45

4. 3,328
    x   25

5. 1,943
    x   56

Multiplication Refresher

Need help explaining to your child how to multiply a four-digit number by a two-digit number with one or more regroupings? Try using the three-step method below. Walk your child through the first problem at the right using this method. Next, have her complete the second problem on her own, verbalizing each step as she solves the problem. Then have her complete the remaining problems independently.

Try using these three steps!

Step 1
Multiply by the ones. Regroup if necessary.

Th	H	T	O	
	1			
1	1	5	2	**Regroup.**
X		4	3	
3	4	5	6	

Step 2
Write a zero to hold the ones place.
Multiply by the tens. Regroup if necessary.

Th	H	T	O	
	2			
	1			
1	1	5	2	**Regroup.**
X		4	3	
	3	4	5	6
4	6	0	8	0

Step 3
Add.

		2			
		1			
	1	1	5	2	
X			4	3	
		1			
	3	4	5	6	
+ 4	6	0	8	0	
4	9,	5	3	6	

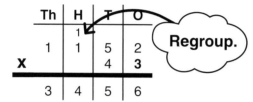

Answers: 49,536; 49,708; 187,515; 83,200; 108,808

If your child is quick to solve the remaining math problems correctly, an occasional review may be all he or she needs. But if several of the answers are incorrect, it's a good idea to spend some time each day having your child work through a problem or two at home until he or she has mastered this skill.

Checkup 6

Name _____   Date _____

A.
$$\begin{array}{r} 2{,}356 \\ \times\ \ 35 \\ \hline \end{array}$$

$$\begin{array}{r} 6{,}581 \\ \times\ \ 62 \\ \hline \end{array}$$

$$\begin{array}{r} 7{,}183 \\ \times\ \ 29 \\ \hline \end{array}$$

B.
$$\begin{array}{r} 5{,}259 \\ \times\ \ 43 \\ \hline \end{array}$$

$$\begin{array}{r} 5{,}264 \\ \times\ \ 27 \\ \hline \end{array}$$

$$\begin{array}{r} 3{,}465 \\ \times\ \ 52 \\ \hline \end{array}$$

C.
$$\begin{array}{r} 6{,}818 \\ \times\ \ 41 \\ \hline \end{array}$$

$$\begin{array}{r} 3{,}056 \\ \times\ \ 29 \\ \hline \end{array}$$

$$\begin{array}{r} 4{,}871 \\ \times\ \ 51 \\ \hline \end{array}$$

Test A: 4 digits x 2 digits with one or more regroupings

©The Education Center, Inc. • *Target Math Success* • TEC60831 • Key p. 136

Checkup 6

Name _____   Date _____

A.
$$\begin{array}{r} 1{,}595 \\ \times\ \ 64 \\ \hline \end{array}$$

$$\begin{array}{r} 1{,}859 \\ \times\ \ 78 \\ \hline \end{array}$$

$$\begin{array}{r} 4{,}732 \\ \times\ \ 76 \\ \hline \end{array}$$

B.
$$\begin{array}{r} 6{,}127 \\ \times\ \ 38 \\ \hline \end{array}$$

$$\begin{array}{r} 9{,}425 \\ \times\ \ 14 \\ \hline \end{array}$$

$$\begin{array}{r} 2{,}678 \\ \times\ \ 59 \\ \hline \end{array}$$

C.
$$\begin{array}{r} 3{,}286 \\ \times\ \ 48 \\ \hline \end{array}$$

$$\begin{array}{r} 8{,}125 \\ \times\ \ 43 \\ \hline \end{array}$$

$$\begin{array}{r} 3{,}084 \\ \times\ \ 85 \\ \hline \end{array}$$

Test B: 4 digits x 2 digits with one or more regroupings

©The Education Center, Inc. • *Target Math Success* • TEC60831 • Key p. 136

It's Time to Take Aim!

On _____ our class will be having a checkup on multiplication of larger numbers. To help your child prepare, please spend about 20 minutes reviewing math problems that involve **multiplying a three-digit number by a three-digit number with one or more regroupings.** Thanks for your help!

Target These!

1. 248
    x 735

2. 627
    x 413

3. 986
    x 234

4. 861
    x 282

5. 776
    x 149

Multiplication Refresher

Need help explaining to your child how to multiply a three-digit number by a three-digit number with one or more regroupings? Try using the four-step method below. Walk your child through the first problem at the right using this method. Next, have him complete the second problem on his own, verbalizing each step as he solves the problem. Then have him complete the remaining problems independently.

Step 1
Multiply by the ones. Regroup if necessary.

Step 2
Write a zero to hold the ones place.
Multiply by the tens. Regroup if necessary.

Step 3
Write a zero to hold the tens place.
Multiply by the hundreds. Regroup if necessary.

Step 4
Add.

Try using these four steps!

H	T	O
3̸	5̸	
1̸	2̸	
2	4	8
X 7	3	5
1		
1 2	4	0
7 4	4	0
1		
+ 1 7 3	6 0	0
1 8 2,	2 8	0

Answers: 182,280; 258,951; 230,724; 242,802; 115,624

If your child is quick to solve the remaining math problems correctly, an occasional review may be all he or she needs. But if several of the answers are incorrect, it's a good idea to spend some time each day having your child work through a problem or two at home until he or she has mastered this skill.

Checkup 7

Name _____

Date _____

A.
```
    847
  x 213
  _____
```

```
    125
  x 692
  _____
```

B.
```
    324
  x 706
  _____
```

```
    652
  x 853
  _____
```

C.
```
    315
  x 976
  _____
```

```
    865
  x 109
  _____
```

Checkup 7

Name _____

Date _____

A.
```
    336
  x 834
  _____
```

```
    261
  x 473
  _____
```

B.
```
    828
  x 803
  _____
```

```
    519
  x 754
  _____
```

C.
```
    256
  x 947
  _____
```

```
    382
  x 855
  _____
```

```
    664
  x 125
  _____
```

```
    670
  x 919
  _____
```

It's Time to Take Aim!

On _____ our class will be having a checkup on multiplication of larger numbers. To help your child prepare, please spend about 20 minutes reviewing math problems that involve **multiplying a four-digit number by a three-digit number with one or more regroupings.** Thanks for your help!

Target These!

1.	1,385
	x 257

2.	3,378
	x 512

Multiplication Refresher

Need help explaining to your child how to multiply a four-digit number by a three-digit number with one or more regroupings? Try using the four-step method below. Walk your child through the first problem at the right using this method. Next, have her complete the second problem on her own, verbalizing each step as she solves the problem. Then have her complete the remaining problems independently.

Try using these four steps!

3.	1,254
	x 437

4.	2,673
	x 356

Step 1
Multiply by the ones. Regroup if necessary.

Step 2
Write a zero to hold the ones place.
Multiply by the tens. Regroup if necessary.

5.	2,941
	x 169

Step 3
Write zeros to hold the ones and tens places.
Multiply by the hundreds. Regroup if necessary.

Step 4
Add.

	Th	H	T	O
		1	1	
	1	4	2	
	2	5	3	
	1,	3	8	5
X		2	5	7
	9	¹6	9	5
² 6	9	2	5	0
¹+ 2	7	7	0	0
3	5	5,	9	4	5

If your child is quick to solve the remaining math problems correctly, an occasional review may be all he or she needs. But if several of the answers are incorrect, it's a good idea to spend some time each day having your child work through a problem or two at home until he or she has mastered this skill.

Checkup 8

Name _____   Date _____

A. 2,714   1,159
    x 326   x 285

B. 2,341   5,326
    x 513   x 253

Test A: 4 digits x 3 digits with one or more regroupings

Checkup 8

Name _____   Date _____

A. 3,982   5,062   8,127
    x 346   x 239   x 249

B. 4,728   1,270   7,933
    x 138   x 342   x 452

Test B: 4 digits x 3 digits with one or more regroupings

Show Your Work

Name _____ Date _____

Show Your Work

Name _____ Date _____

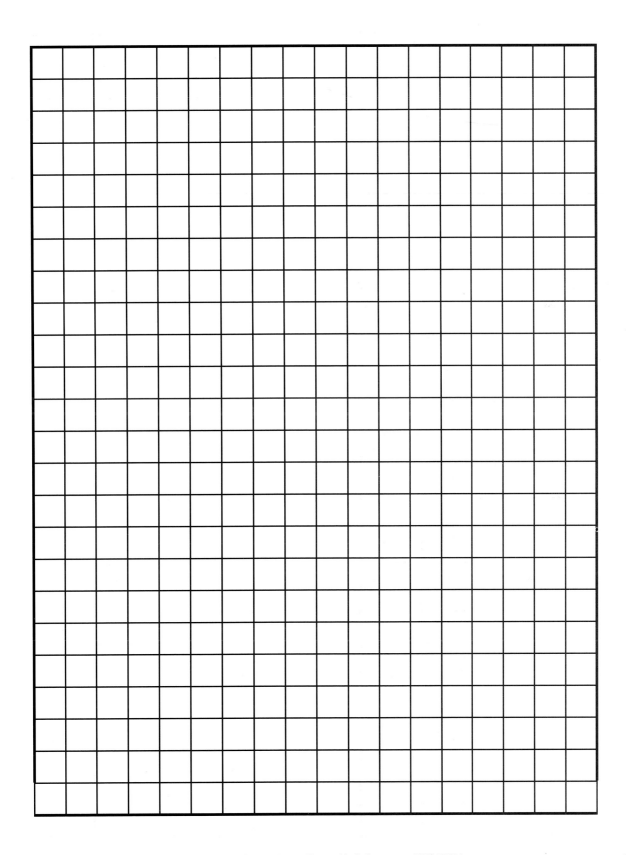

Congratulations!

_____

knows how to

multiply by

1 digit!

You hit the multiplication target!

Multiplying by **1** Digit Award

_____
Teacher

_____
Date

Congratulations!

You've had great target practice!

_____

knows how to

multiply by

2 digits!

Multiplying by 2 Digits Award

_____
Teacher

_____
Date

Congratulations!

_____

knows how to

multiply by

3 digits!

Multiplying
by
3 Digits
Award

You
really hit
the mark!

_____
Teacher

_____
Date

Path to the Party

Multiply.
Color the boxes with answers greater than 50 to show the path.

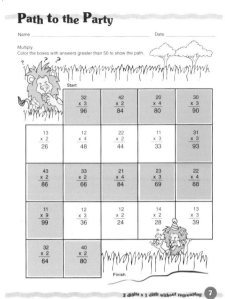

Start

32 x 3 = 96	42 x 2 = 84	20 x 4 = 80	30 x 3 = 90
13 x 2 = 26	12 x 4 = 48	22 x 2 = 44	11 x 3 = 33	31 x 3 = 93
43 x 2 = 86	33 x 2 = 66	21 x 4 = 84	23 x 3 = 69	22 x 4 = 88
11 x 9 = 99	12 x 3 = 36	12 x 2 = 24	14 x 2 = 28	13 x 3 = 39
32 x 2 = 64	40 x 2 = 80			

Finish

2 digits x 1 digit without regrouping 7

Play Ball!

Read.
Solve each problem on another sheet of paper.
Write the answer in the blank.

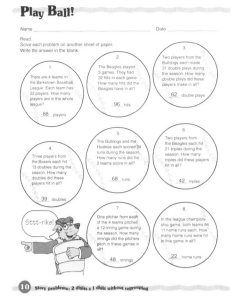

1. There are 4 teams in the Barkstown Baseball League. Each team has 22 players. How many players are in the whole league?
88 players

2. The Beagles played 3 games. They had 32 hits in each game. How many hits did the Beagles have in all?
96 hits

3. Two players from the Bulldogs each made 31 double plays during the season. How many double plays did these players make in all?
62 double plays

4. Three players from the Boxers each hit 13 doubles during the season. How many doubles did these players hit in all?
39 doubles

5. The Bulldogs and the Huskies each scored 34 runs during the season. How many runs did the 2 teams score in all?
68 runs

6. Two players from the Beagles each hit 21 triples during the season. How many triples did these players hit in all?
42 triples

7. One pitcher from each of the 4 teams pitched a 12-inning game during the season. How many innings did the pitchers pitch in these games in all?
48 innings

8. In the league championship game, both teams hit 11 home runs each. How many home runs were hit in this game in all?
22 home runs

Sttt-rike!

Story problems; 2 digits x 1 digit without regrouping 10

Clarabell's Crossing

Multiply.
Show your work.
To solve the riddle, match the letters to the numbered lines below.

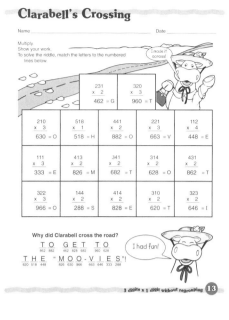

I made it across!

| 231 x 2 = 462 = G | 320 x 3 = 960 = T |

210 x 3 = 630 = O	518 x 1 = 518 = H	441 x 2 = 882 = O	221 x 3 = 663 = V	112 x 4 = 448 = E
111 x 3 = 333 = E	413 x 2 = 826 = M	341 x 2 = 682 = T	314 x 2 = 628 = O	431 x 2 = 862 = T
322 x 3 = 966 = O	144 x 2 = 288 = S	414 x 2 = 828 = E	310 x 2 = 620 = T	323 x 2 = 646 = I

Why did Clarabell cross the road?

T O G E T T O
862 628 620   682 628 620

T H E "M O O - V I E S"!
620 518 448   826 630 966 663 646 454 333 288

I had fun!

3 digits x 1 digit without regrouping 13

Fancy Fish

Multiply.
Color by the code.

Color Code
0–25 = green
26–50 = yellow
51–75 = orange
76–100 = blue

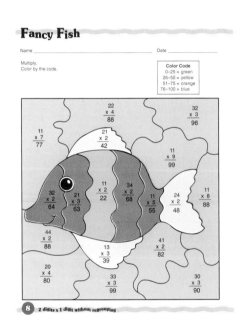

22 x 4 = 88
32 x 3 = 96
11 x 7 = 77
21 x 2 = 42
11 x 9 = 99
32 x 2 = 64
21 x 3 = 63
11 x 2 = 22
34 x 2 = 68
11 x 5 = 55
24 x 2 = 48
11 x 8 = 88
44 x 2 = 88
13 x 3 = 39
41 x 2 = 82
20 x 4 = 80
33 x 3 = 99
30 x 3 = 90

2 digits x 1 digit without regrouping 8

Mail Me!

Multiply.
Show your work.
To show the path to the mailbox, color the envelopes whose answers are less than 450.

Start

Hurry! The mailman is on the way!

213 x 2 = 426	123 x 2 = 246	321 x 2 = 642
301 x 2 = 602	133 x 3 = 399	231 x 3 = 693	233 x 3 = 699
123 x 3 = 369	234 x 2 = 468	321 x 3 = 963	203 x 3 = 609
211 x 2 = 422	132 x 3 = 396		
312 x 3 = 936	332 x 3 = 996		

3 digits x 1 digit without regrouping 11

Trudy's Travel Troubles

Read.
Solve each problem on another sheet of paper.
Write the answer in the blank.

1. When Trudy visited Australia, she lost the candy mints she bought. She lost 111 mints each day for 8 days. How many mints did she lose in all?
888 mints

2. Trudy tried to make leis in Hawaii but damaged the flowers. She damaged 110 flowers each of the 6 days she was there. How many flowers did she damage in all?
660 flowers

3. Trudy liked drinking tea in England, but she had trouble holding the cups. She dropped 3 teacups each day for 101 days. How many teacups did she drop in all?
303 teacups

4. In France Trudy kept forgetting the names of famous artists. She forgot 112 names at 4 different art galleries. How many names did she forget in all?
448 names

5. In Egypt Trudy tripped on steps at the pyramids. She tripped 102 times at 4 different pyramids. How many times did she trip in all?
408 times

6. In Mexico Trudy sometimes spoke French instead of Spanish. She spoke French 211 times in 4 different towns. How many times did she speak French in all?
844 times

7. Trudy went skiing in Switzerland. She fell 9 times on each of the 100 days she was there. How many times did she fall in all?
900 times

Trouble follows me around.

Story problems; 3 digits x 1 digit without regrouping 14

Take Flight

Multiply.
Cross off each answer on the runway.
Some numbers will not be crossed off.

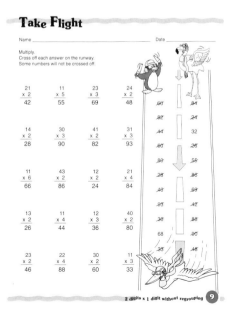

21 x 2 = 42	11 x 5 = 55	23 x 3 = 69	24 x 2 = 48
14 x 2 = 28	30 x 3 = 90	41 x 2 = 82	31 x 3 = 93
11 x 6 = 66	43 x 2 = 86	12 x 2 = 24	21 x 4 = 84
13 x 2 = 26	11 x 4 = 44	12 x 3 = 36	40 x 2 = 80
23 x 2 = 46	22 x 4 = 88	30 x 2 = 60	11 x 3 = 33

66 84
82 24
44 26
60 58
48 69
93 42
38 88
68 90
33 48

2 digits x 1 digit without regrouping 9

Gotta Have a Gumball!

Multiply.
Show your work.
Color by the code.

| Between 0 and 300 | Between 301 and 600 | Between 601 and 1,000 |
| Pink | Yellow | Blue |

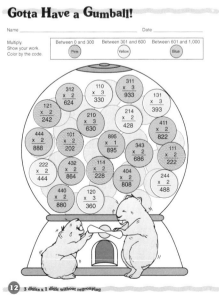

312 x 2 = 624
110 x 3 = 330
311 x 3 = 933
131 x 3 = 393
121 x 2 = 242
210 x 3 = 630
214 x 2 = 428
411 x 2 = 822
444 x 2 = 888
101 x 2 = 202
895 x 1 = 895
343 x 2 = 686
111 x 2 = 222
222 x 2 = 444
432 x 2 = 864
114 x 2 = 228
404 x 2 = 808
244 x 2 = 488
440 x 2 = 880
120 x 3 = 360

3 digits x 1 digit without regrouping 12

Fancy Feathers

Multiply.
Color by the code.

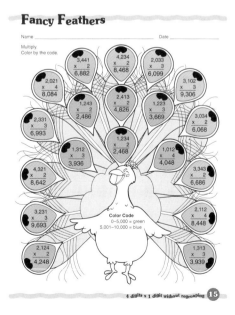

3,441 x 2 = 6,882
4,234 x 2 = 8,468
2,033 x 3 = 6,099
2,021 x 4 = 8,084
3,102 x 3 = 9,306
1,243 x 2 = 2,486
2,413 x 2 = 4,826
1,223 x 3 = 3,669
3,034 x 2 = 6,068
2,331 x 3 = 6,993
1,234 x 2 = 2,468
1,312 x 3 = 3,936
1,012 x 4 = 4,048
4,321 x 2 = 8,642
3,343 x 2 = 6,686
3,231 x 3 = 9,693
2,112 x 4 = 8,448
2,124 x 2 = 4,248
1,313 x 3 = 3,939

Color Code
0–5,000 = green
5,001–10,000 = blue

4 digits x 1 digit without regrouping 15

Goin' Fishin'

Name _____ Date _____

Multiply.
Show your work on another sheet of paper.
Color each correct answer. Connect the colored boxes to draw a path to the fishing hole.

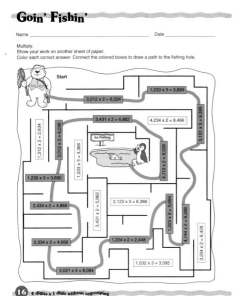

Start

3,012 x 2 = 6,024
1,233 x 3 = 3,699
3,431 x 2 = 6,862
4,234 x 2 = 8,466
1,312 x 2 = 2,634
2,033 x 3 = 6,206
Ice Fishing
3,131 x 3 = 3,393
1,033 x 3 = 3,366
4,113 x 2 = 8,226
1,230 x 3 = 3,690
2,123 x 3 = 6,366
1,223 x 3 = 3,669
2,434 x 2 = 4,868
3,431 x 2 = 5,862
1,223 x 3 = 8,288
2,334 x 2 = 4,668
1,224 x 2 = 2,448
4,144 x 2 = 6,428
2,021 x 4 = 8,084
1,032 x 3 = 3,095
3,204 x 2 = 6,428

16 4 digits x 1 digit without regrouping

Up, Up, and Away!

Name _____ Date _____

Multiply.
Show your work.
Cross off each matching answer on the balloon.
Some numbers will not be crossed off.

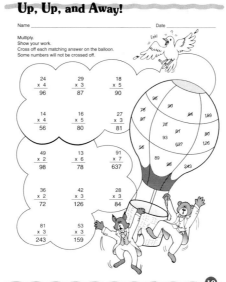

```
  24        29        18
 x 4       x 3       x 5
 ___       ___       ___
  96        87        90

  14        16        27
 x 4       x 5       x 3
 ___       ___       ___
  56        80        81

  49        13        91
 x 2       x 6       x 7
 ___       ___       ___
  98        78       637

  36        42        28
 x 2       x 3       x 3
 ___       ___       ___
  72       126        84

  81        53
 x 3       x 3
 ___       ___
 243       159
```

Balloon numbers: 96, 56, 90, 84, 189, 78, 81, 93, 91, 90, 56, 637, 126, 89, 96, 243

2 digits x 1 digit with one regrouping 19

Such Silly Seals!

Name _____ Date _____

Read.
Solve each problem on another sheet of paper.
Write the answer in the blank.

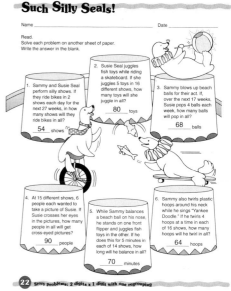

1. Sammy and Susie Seal perform silly shows. If they ride bikes in 2 shows each day for the next 27 weeks, in how many shows will they ride bikes in all?
   54 shows

2. Susie Seal juggles fish toys while riding a skateboard. If she juggles 5 toys in 16 different shows, how many toys will she juggle in all?
   80 toys

3. Sammy blows up beach balls for their act. If, over the next 17 weeks, Susie pops 4 balls each week, how many balls will pop in all?
   68 balls

4. At 15 different shows, 6 people each wanted to take a picture of Susie. If Susie crosses her eyes in the pictures, how many people in all will get cross-eyed pictures?
   90 people

5. While Sammy balances a beach ball on his nose, he stands on one front flipper and juggles fish toys in the other. If he does this for 5 minutes in each of 14 shows, how long will he balance in all?
   70 minutes

6. Sammy also twirls plastic hoops around his neck while he sings "Yankee Doodle." If he twirls 4 hoops at a time in each of 16 shows, how many hoops will he twirl in all?
   64 hoops

22 Story problems; 2 digits x 1 digit with one regrouping

Spotted Snacker

Name _____ Date _____

Multiply.
Show your work on another sheet of paper.
To solve the riddle, match the letters to the numbered lines below.

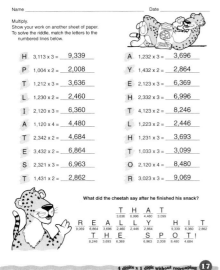

```
H  3,113 x 3 =  9,339        A  1,232 x 3 =  3,696
P  1,004 x 2 =  2,008        Y  1,432 x 2 =  2,864
T  1,212 x 3 =  3,636        E  2,123 x 3 =  6,369
L  1,230 x 2 =  2,460        H  2,332 x 3 =  6,996
I  2,120 x 3 =  6,360        T  4,123 x 2 =  8,246
A  1,120 x 4 =  4,480        L  1,223 x 2 =  2,446
T  2,342 x 2 =  4,684        H  1,231 x 3 =  3,693
E  3,432 x 2 =  6,864        T  1,033 x 3 =  3,099
S  2,321 x 3 =  6,963        O  2,120 x 4 =  8,480
T  1,431 x 2 =  2,862        R  3,023 x 3 =  9,069
```

What did the cheetah say after he finished his snack?

T H A T
3,636 9,339 4,480 3,099

R E A L L Y   H I T
9,069 6,864 3,696 2,460 2,446 2,864   9,339 6,360 3,636

T H E   S P O T !
8,246 3,693 6,369   6,963 2,008 8,480 4,684

17 4 digits x 1 digit without regrouping

Catching Anything?

Name _____ Date _____

Multiply.
Show your work.
Color each fish that has a matching answer.

```
 27      18      13      90      21      41
x 3     x 5     x 6     x 5     x 7     x 5
___     ___     ___     ___     ___     ___
 81      90      78     450     147     205

 72      35      14      38      83      25
x 4     x 2     x 6     x 2     x 3     x 3
___     ___     ___     ___     ___     ___
288      70      84      76     249      75

 46      93      28      16      91      32
x 2     x 3     x 2     x 6     x 9     x 4
___     ___     ___     ___     ___     ___
 92     279      56      96     819     128

 40      61
x 5     x 4
___     ___
200     244
```

Fish answers: 88, 249, 78, 84, 205, 819, 200, 81, 450, 75, 244, 288, 279, 56, 128, 92, 54, 70, 76, 90, 96, 147

20 2 digits x 1 digit with one regrouping

Fresh From the Honeycomb

Name _____ Date _____

Multiply.
Show your work.

```
 307      219      127      324
x 2      x 4      x 3      x 3
___      ___      ___      ___
614      876      381      972

245      141      128      253
x 2      x 5      x 3      x 2
___      ___      ___      ___
490      705      384      506

315      192      120
x 2      x 4      x 8
___      ___      ___
630      768      960

116      346      263
x 6      x 2      x 3
___      ___      ___
696      692      789
```

23 3 digits x 1 digit with one regrouping

Sweet Shop

Name _____ Date _____

Read.
Solve each problem on another sheet of paper.
Write the answer in the blank.

TASTYTOWN Sweet Shop

1. The Tastytown Sweet Shop sells 2,412 chocolate pops each month. How many chocolate pops will the shop sell in 2 months?
   4,824 chocolate pops

2. The Sweet Shop's owner orders 2,032 bags of jelly beans each year. In 3 years, how many bags of jelly beans will he have ordered in all?
   6,096 bags

3. Each week the owner refills the gumball machine with 1,211 gumballs. How many gumballs will he put in the machine in 4 weeks?
   4,844 gumballs

4. The Sweet Shop customers buy 3,123 fruit chews each month. How many fruit chews will customers buy in 3 months?
   9,369 fruit chews

5. The Too Sweet Sugar Company delivers 1,021 pounds of sugar to the shop each week. After 4 weeks, how many pounds of sugar will they have delivered in all?
   4,084 pounds

6. The workers at the shop made 4,432 pieces of candy last month. If they make the same amount of candy each month for 2 months, how many pieces of candy will they make in all?
   8,864 pieces

18 Story problems; 4 digits x 1 digit without regrouping

What's Wally Watching?

Name _____ Date _____

Multiply.
Show your work on another sheet of paper.
Color the boxes with correct answers to show the path to the TV show.

61 x 8 =	148	468	489	488
25 x 2 =	47	40	50	57
17 x 3 =	54	51	61	64
24 x 4 =	68	96	84	64
26 x 3 =	78	69	59	68
28 x 2 =	56	50	46	40
31 x 9 =	270	279	260	269
36 x 2 =	62	52	72	78
12 x 8 =	80	86	90	96
23 x 4 =	67	82	92	87
12 x 5 =	70	60	50	57
18 x 2 =	36	30	46	26
12 x 7 =	79	84	89	74
14 x 7 =	91	98	78	96
51 x 4 =	205	201	204	94

Walrus World | Tips on Tusks | 100 Ways to Eat Clams | Ice Floe Tricks

21 2 digits x 1 digit with one regrouping

Just Like Home!

Name _____ Date _____

Multiply.
Show your work.
To solve the riddle, match the letters to the numbered lines below.

```
          108       446       118
         x 5       x 2       x 3
         ___       ___       ___
218      540 = E   892 = O   354 = R
x 4
___
872 = O

306               140       291       107
x 2              x 6       x 3       x 6
___              ___       ___       ___
612 = A          840 = V   873 = I   642 = T

153
x 3
___
459 = G

482      339       105       328
x 2      x 2      x 7      x 3
___      ___      ___      ___
964 = M  678 = L   735 = R   984 = H

         260
         x 3
         ___
         780 = L

214
x 4
___
856 = E   217
         x 4
         ___
         868 = H

381
x 2
___
762 = E

104
x 4
___
416 = T
```

Where did the baseball player pitch his tent?

R I G H T
354 873 459 984 642

O V E R
872 840 856 735

H O M E
868 892 964 540

P L A T E !
762 780 678 416 540

24 3 digits x 1 digit with one regrouping

127

Help Me Down!

Name _____ Date _____

Multiply.
Show your work on another sheet of paper.
Color each rock with a correct answer to show the path down the rocks.

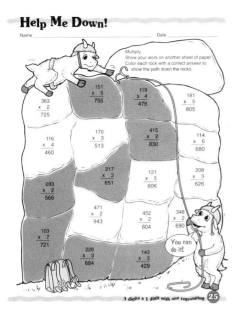

151
× 5
755

119
× 4
476

181
× ?
805

363
× 2
725

116
× 4
460

170
× 3
513

415
× ?
830

114
× 6
680

283
× 2
566

217
× 3
651

121
× 5
606

208
× 3
626

471
× 2
943

452
× 2
804

348
× 2
690

103
× 7
721

228
× 3
684

143
× 3
429

You can do it!

3 digits x 1 digit with one regrouping   25

Where's All the Booty Buried?

Name _____ Date _____

Multiply.
Show your work on another sheet of paper.
If correct, color the island green.
If incorrect, color the island blue.
The treasure is on the green islands.

1,103
× 6
6,618

1,307
× 3
3,921

2,194
× 2
4,386

1,181
× 4
4,724

2,216
× 4
8,864

3,439
× 2
6,878

1,416
× 2
2,722

3,110
× 8
24,880

3,372
× 2
5,644

2,402
× 3
7,206

1,091
× 6
6,546

1,812
× 4
7,446

3,513
× 2
7,026

1,006
× 6
6,036

6,001
× 7
42,007

1,031
× 5
5,055

4 digits x 1 digit with one regrouping   28

Paint Job

Name _____ Date _____

Multiply.
Show your work.
Color by the code.

How's it looking?

58
× 6
348

73
× 7
511

34
× 5
170

49
× 3
147

45
× 7
315

67
× 5
335

38
× 3
114

88
× 6
528

29
× 4
116

64
× 8
512

93
× 4
372

19
× 8
152

83
× 9
747

26
× 6
156

37
× 7
259

74
× 8
592

87
× 3
261

72
× 4
288

97
× 3
291

95
× 6
570

24
× 9
216

Lookin' good!

Code
100–250 = red
251–500 = yellow
501–750 = green

2 digits x 1 digit with one or more regroupings   31

Ellie's Jungle Mart

Name _____ Date _____

Read.
Solve each problem on another sheet of paper.
Write the answer in the blank.

1. Ellie stocked 2 shelves with tree branches. She put 105 branches on each shelf. How many branches did she stock in all?

   210 branches

2. There are 3 shelves for strips of bark. Each shelf holds 282 strips. How many strips of bark will the shelves hold in all?

   846 strips of bark

3. Sugarcane bundles are on sale. Ellie sold 113 bundles. Each bundle holds 6 sugarcane stalks. How many stalks did Ellie sell in all?

   678 stalks

4. Today 224 elephants came through Ellie's express lane. Each elephant bought 4 items. How many total items were sold to elephants in the express lane today?

   896 items

5. One case of coconuts holds 8. Ellie moved 121 cases. How many coconuts did she move in all?

   968 coconuts

6. If Ellie sells 191 gallons of milk each week, how many gallons of milk will she sell in 5 weeks?

   955 gallons of milk

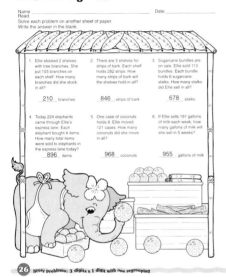

26 Story problems: 3 digits x 1 digit with one regrouping

Aim for the Green!

Name _____ Date _____

Multiply.
Show your work.
Cross off the matching answer on the trees.
Some numbers will not be crossed off.

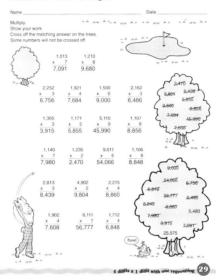

1,013
× 7
7,091

1,210
× 8
9,680

2,252
× 3
6,756

1,921
× 4
7,684

1,500
× 6
9,000

2,162
× 3
6,486

1,305
× 3
3,915

1,171
× 5
5,855

5,110
× 9
45,990

1,107
× 8
8,856

1,140
× 7
7,980

1,235
× 2
2,470

9,011
× 6
54,066

1,106
× 8
8,848

2,813
× 3
8,439

4,902
× 2
9,804

2,215
× 4
8,860

1,902
× 4
7,608

8,111
× 7
56,777

1,712
× 4
6,848

Trees (crossed off answers):
7,091 9,680
2,470 8,439
9,804 9,855
9,680 8,855
7,684 7,980

9,000
54,066 6,756
8,848 8,860
56,777 5,485
8,848 8,860
7,980 5,480
3,915 7,091
25,575

Fore!

4 digits x 1 digit with one regrouping   29

All Ears!

Name _____ Date _____

Multiply.
Show your work.
Write each answer in the square below. The sum of each row and column should be 1,000.

1. 48 × 3 = 144
2. 62 × 5 = 310
3. 56 × 4 = 224
4. 46 × 7 = 322
5. 72 × 7 = 504
6. 39 × 5 = 195
7. 37 × 3 = 111
8. 38 × 5 = 190
9. 19 × 8 = 152
10. 37 × 9 = 333
11. 45 × 9 = 405
12. 22 × 5 = 110
13. 25 × 8 = 200
14. 18 × 9 = 162
15. 52 × 5 = 260
16. 63 × 6 = 378

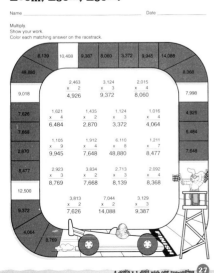

144	310	224	322
504	195	111	190
152	333	405	110
200	162	260	378

32 2 digits x 1 digit with one or more regroupings

Zoom, Zoom, Zoom!

Name _____ Date _____

Multiply.
Show your work.
Color each matching answer on the racetrack.

8,139 10,408 9,387 8,060 3,372 9,945 14,088
48,880   8,368
9,018   7,998
7,626   4,926
7,668   6,484
2,870   7,648
8,477
12,500
9,372
4,064
8,769

2,463
× 2
4,926

3,124
× 3
9,372

2,015
× 4
8,060

1,621
× 4
6,484

1,435
× 2
2,870

1,124
× 3
3,372

1,016
× 4
4,064

1,105
× 9
9,945

1,912
× 4
7,648

6,110
× 8
48,880

1,211
× 7
8,477

2,923
× 3
8,769

3,834
× 2
7,668

2,713
× 3
8,139

2,092
× 4
8,368

3,813
× 2
7,626

7,044
× 2
14,088

3,129
× 3
9,387

4 digits x 1 digit with one regrouping   27

Got Plumbing Problems?

Name _____ Date _____

Read.
Solve each problem on another sheet of paper.
Write the answer in the blank.
To solve the riddle, write the letter of each answer in its matching numbered blank below.

1. The Lily Pad plumbers are busy. They fixed 1,018 broken pipes last month. At this rate, how many pipes will these plumbers fix in 3 months?

   3,054 pipes = O

2. Drippy faucets are also a big problem. The plumbers fixed 1,160 of them last month. At this rate, how many drippy faucets will the plumbers fix in 6 months?

   6,960 faucets = C

3. Another problem is stopped-up drains. The plumbers repaired 1,106 of them last month. At this rate, how many drains will the plumbers repair in 9 months?

   9,954 drains = L

4. Some folks want the plumbers to put in new water heaters. If the plumbers put in 1,253 heaters each month, how many will they put in 2 months?

   2,506 water heaters = S

5. Other folks need new water pumps. If the plumbers put in 1,004 pumps each month, how many will they install in 8 months?

   8,032 pumps = G

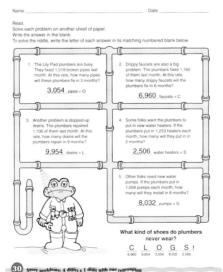

What kind of shoes do plumbers never wear?

C L O G S !
6,960 9,954 3,054 8,032 2,506

30 Story problems: 4 digits x 1 digit with one regrouping

Got Ya!

Name _____ Date _____

Multiply.
Show your work.
Cross off each answer on the boots.
Some numbers will not be crossed off.

17
× 8
136

27
× 5
135

33
× 4
132

74
× 3
222

39
× 8
312

46
× 6
276

24
× 7
168

54
× 5
270

65
× 7
455

69
× 3
207

77
× 7
539

57
× 4
228

48
× 4
192

55
× 7
385

82
× 9
738

94
× 3
282

44
× 5
220

16
× 9
144

81
× 8
648

92
× 6
552

244   126

2 digits x 1 digit with one or more regroupings   33

Beep! Beep!

Multiply.
Show your work on another sheet of paper.

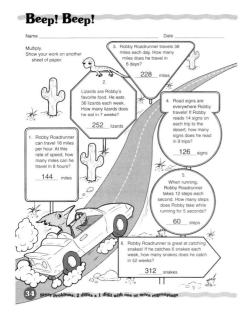

3. Robby Roadrunner travels 38 miles each day. How many miles does he travel in 6 days?

228 miles

Lizards are Robby's favorite food. He eats 36 lizards each week. How many lizards does he eat in 7 weeks?

252 lizards

4. Road signs are everywhere Robby travels! If Robby reads 14 signs on each trip to the desert, how many signs does he read in 9 trips?

126 signs

1. Robby Roadrunner can travel 18 miles per hour. At this rate of speed, how many miles can he travel in 8 hours?

144 miles

5. When running, Robby Roadrunner takes 12 steps each second. How many steps does Robby take while running for 5 seconds?

60 steps

6. Robby Roadrunner is great at catching snakes! If he catches 6 snakes each week, how many snakes does he catch in 52 weeks?

312 snakes

34 Story problems: 2 digits x 1 digit with one or more regroupings

---

Tooth Alert!

Multiply.
Show your work on another sheet of paper.
Color by the code to solve the riddle.

Color Code
Answer starting with 3–9 = yellow
Answer starting with 2 = blue
Answer starting with 1 = red

What two letters are bad for your teeth?

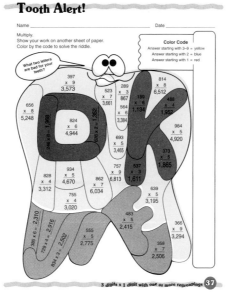

```
397      289      814
 x 9      x 3      x 8
3,573            6,512

523      189      488
 x 7      x 6      x 4
3,661   1,134   1,952

656      564      984
 x 8      x 2      x 5
5,248   1,128   4,920

824              693
 x 6              x 5
4,944           3,465

934      757      537      373
 x 5      x 9      x 3      x 5
4,670   6,813   1,611   1,865

828      862              639
 x 4      x 7              x 5
3,312   6,034           3,195

755              483      366
 x 4              x 5      x 9
3,020           2,415   3,294

386 x 6 = 2,310          358
729 x 4 = 2,916          x 7
834 x 3 = 2,502  555     2,506
                  x 5
                 2,775
```

37

3 digits x 1 digit with one or more regroupings

Pencil Pals

Multiply.
Show your work on another sheet of paper.
Match the letters to the numbered lines below to solve the riddle.

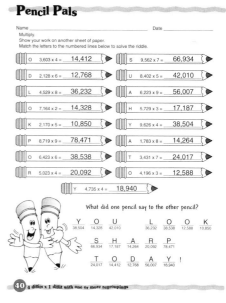

O	3,603 x 4 = **14,412**	S	9,562 x 7 = **66,934**
D	2,128 x 6 = **12,768**	U	8,402 x 5 = **42,010**
L	4,529 x 8 = **36,232**	A	6,223 x 9 = **56,007**
O	7,164 x 2 = **14,328**	H	5,729 x 3 = **17,187**
K	2,170 x 5 = **10,850**	Y	9,626 x 4 = **38,504**
P	8,719 x 9 = **78,471**	A	1,783 x 8 = **14,264**
O	6,423 x 6 = **38,538**	T	3,431 x 7 = **24,017**
R	5,023 x 4 = **20,092**	O	4,196 x 3 = **12,588**

Y 4,735 x 4 = **18,940**

What did one pencil say to the other pencil?

Y O U   L O O K
38,504 14,328 42,010   36,232 12,588 10,850

S H A R P
66,934 17,187 14,264 20,092 78,471

T O D A Y !
24,017 14,412 12,768 56,007 18,940

40 4 digits x 1 digit with one or more regroupings

What's the Very Important Date?

Multiply.
Show your work.
To show the path to the event, color the clocks whose answers end in 5, 6, or 8.

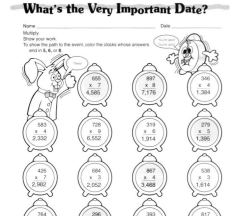

```
655      897      346
 x 7      x 8      x 4
4,585   7,176   1,384

583      728      319      279
 x 4      x 9      x 6      x 5
2,332   6,552   1,914   1,395

426      684      867      538
 x 7      x 3      x 4      x 3
2,982   2,052   3,468   1,614

764      296      393      817
 x 5      x 8      x 4      x 9
3,820   2,368   1,572   7,353
```

eat carrot soup with Alice

play cards with the Queen of Hearts

buy a hat for the Mad Hatter

take catnip to the Cheshire Cat

35 3 digits x 1 digit with one or more regroupings

Roscoe's Roundup!

Read.
Solve each problem on another sheet of paper.
Write the answer in the blank.
To solve the riddle, write the letter of each answer in its matching numbered blank below.

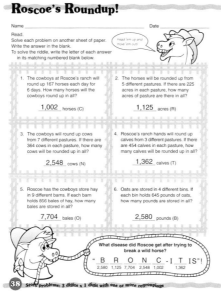

1. The cowboys at Roscoe's ranch will round up 167 horses each day for 6 days. How many horses will the cowboys round up in all?

1,002 horses (C)

2. The horses will be rounded up from 5 different pastures. If there are 225 acres in each pasture, how many acres of pasture are there in all?

1,125 acres (R)

3. The cowboys will round up cows from 7 different pastures. If there are 364 cows in each pasture, how many cows will be rounded up in all?

2,548 cows (N)

4. Roscoe's ranch hands will round up calves from 3 different pastures. If there are 454 calves in each pasture, how many calves will be rounded up in all?

1,362 calves (T)

5. Roscoe has the cowboys store hay in 9 different barns. If each barn holds 856 bales of hay, how many bales are stored in all?

7,704 bales (O)

6. Oats are stored in 4 different bins. If each bin holds 645 pounds of oats, how many pounds are stored in all?

2,580 pounds (B)

What disease did Roscoe get after trying to break a wild horse?

" B R O N C - I T I S "!
   2,580 1,125 7,704 2,548 1,362

38 Story problems: 3 digits x 1 digit with one or more regroupings

---

Route to the Loot

Multiply.
Show your work on another sheet of paper.
Color if correct.
Connect the colored boxes to draw a path to the treasure chest.

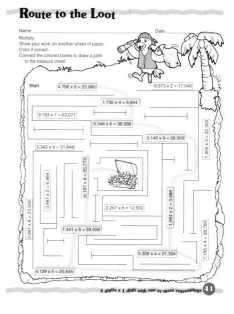

```
Start   4,796 x 5 = 23,980        8,573 x 2 = 17,046

                 1,736 x 4 = 6,944

9,153 x 7 = 63,071      6,348 x 6 = 38,088

                 3,145 x 9 = 28,305   7,455 x 3 = 22,365

5,343 x 6 = 31,848

3,487 x 2 = 6,984    6,197 x 9 = 55,773

2,941 x 8 = 23,328   2,267 x 6 = 12,602   1,994 x 2 = 3,988

                 7,441 x 8 = 59,528   7,195 x 4 = 28,780

                 5,326 x 4 = 21,304

4,129 x 5 = 20,645
```

41 4 digits x 1 digit with one or more regroupings

Football Fever!

Multiply.
Show your work on another sheet of paper.
Color if correct.
Connect the colored footballs to show the path to the goal.

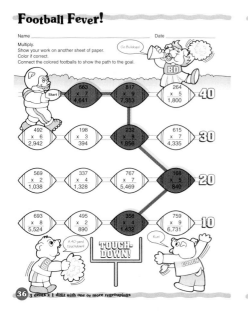

```
Start
663      817      264
 x 7      x 9      x 5
4,641   7,353   1,800                40

492      198      232      615
 x 6      x 3      x 8      x 7
2,942    394    1,856   4,335        30

569      337      767      168
 x 2      x 4      x 7      x 5
1,038   1,328   5,469    840         20

693      495      358      759
 x 8      x 2      x 4      x 9
5,524    890    1,432   6,731        10
```

TOUCH-DOWN!

36 3 digits x 1 digit with one or more regroupings

Beach Blanket

Multiply.
Show your work.
Color by the code.

Color Code
0–20,000 = purple
20,001–40,000 = green
40,001–60,000 = yellow
60,001–80,000 = orange
80,001–100,000 = red

```
9,725      1,476
 x 3        x 4
29,175     5,904

8,824   8,451   8,354   6,613
 x 2     x 6     x 9     x 5
15,744  50,706  75,186  33,065

                9,965
                 x 9
                89,685

7,026                   5,728
 x 4                     x 2
28,104                  11,456

       9,033      7,922
        x 7        x 7
       63,231     55,454

6,179      4,921
 x 3        x 8
18,537     39,368
```

39 4 digits x 1 digit with one or more regroupings

On the Go

Read.
Solve each problem on another sheet of paper.
Write the answer in the blank.

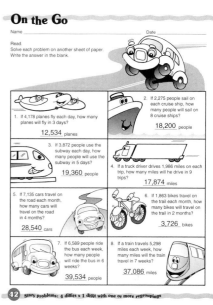

1. If 4,178 planes fly each day, how many planes will fly in 3 days?

12,534 planes

2. If 2,275 people sail on each cruise ship, how many people will sail on 8 cruise ships?

18,200 people

3. If 3,872 people use the subway each day, how many people will use the subway in 5 days?

19,360 people

4. If a truck driver drives 1,986 miles on each trip, how many miles will he drive in 9 trips?

17,874 miles

5. If 7,135 cars travel on the road each month, how many cars will travel on the road in 4 months?

28,540 cars

6. If 1,863 bikes travel on the trail each month, how many bikes will travel on the trail in 2 months?

3,726 bikes

7. If 6,589 people ride the bus each week, how many people will ride the bus in 6 weeks?

39,534 people

8. If a train travels 5,298 miles each week, how many miles will the train travel in 7 weeks?

37,086 miles

42 Story problems: 4 digits x 1 digit with one or more regroupings

---

129

Who's Minding the Castle?

Multiply.
Show your work.
Cross off the matching answer on the castle door.
Some numbers will not be crossed off.

31 x 23	13 x 13	17 x 11	42 x 20	21 x 14
713	169	187	840	294

37 x 11	14 x 12	41 x 12	33 x 13
407	168	492	429

32 x 21	40
672	880

34 x 21	29 x 11
714	319

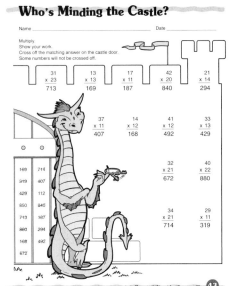

169 714
319 407
429 112
850 840
713 187
880 294
168 492
672

2 digits x 2 digits without regrouping **43**

Way Cool Music

Read.
Solve each problem on another sheet of paper.
Write the answer in the blank.

1. I. C. Ice made 14 CDs. Each CD has 21 songs. How many songs are there in all?
294 songs

2. I. C. wrote 22 songs for his last CD. He spent 43 minutes writing each song. How many minutes did it take I. C. to write the songs in all?
946 minutes

3. I. C. ordered 31 cartons of T-shirts to give away at his first concert. Each carton has 12 shirts. How many shirts will he give away in all?
372 shirts

4. I. C. will visit 11 music stores to promote his new CD. He has agreed to sign 35 autographs at each store. How many autographs will he sign in all?
385 autographs

5. I. C.'s concert is sold out! A ticket was sold for every seat. There are 44 rows of seats. Each row has 20 seats. How many tickets were sold to I. C.'s concert?
880 tickets

6. I. C. and his group drink 13 bottles of water at every concert. They have 23 concerts. How many bottles of water will they need?
299 bottles of water

I. C. Ice SOLD OUT!

Story problems: 2 digits x 2 digits without regrouping **46**

The Buzz About Baseball

Multiply.
Show your work on another sheet of paper.
Color each space that contains a correct answer.

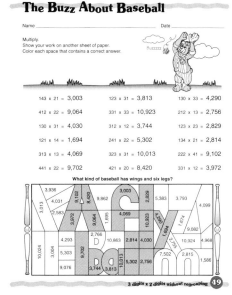

Buzzzzzz

143 x 21 = 3,003	123 x 31 = 3,813	130 x 33 = 4,290
412 x 22 = 9,064	331 x 33 = 10,923	212 x 13 = 2,756
130 x 31 = 4,030	312 x 12 = 3,744	123 x 23 = 2,829
121 x 14 = 1,694	241 x 22 = 5,302	134 x 21 = 2,814
313 x 13 = 4,069	323 x 31 = 10,013	222 x 41 = 9,102
441 x 22 = 9,702	421 x 20 = 8,420	331 x 12 = 3,972

What kind of baseball has wings and six legs?

3 digits x 2 digits without regrouping **49**

One-Stop Shopping

Multiply.
Show your work on another sheet of paper.
Color boxes with correct answers to show the path to the outlet.

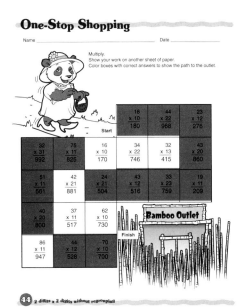

18 x 10 = 180	44 x 22 = 968	23 x 12 = 276

Start

32 x 31 = 992	75 x 11 = 825	16 x 10 = 170	34 x 22 = 746	32 x 13 = 415	43 x 20 = 860
51 x 11 = 561	42 x 21 = 881	24 x 21 = 504	43 x 12 = 516	33 x 23 = 759	19 x 11 = 209
40 x 20 = 800	37 x 11 = 517	62 x 10 = 730			
86 x 11 = 947	44 x 12 = 528	70 x 10 = 700			

Bamboo Outlet
Finish

2 digits x 2 digits without regrouping **44**

Snake in the Grass

Multiply.
Show your work.
Color by the code.

Color Code
0–3,000 = red
3,001–6,000 = yellow
6,001–9,000 = gray
9,001–12,000 = green

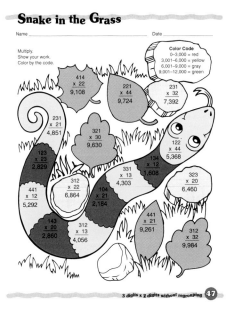

414 x 22 = 9,108
231 x 44 = 9,724
231 x 32 = 7,392
231 x 21 = 4,851
321 x 30 = 9,630
122 x 44 = 5,368
123 x 23 = 2,829
331 x 13 = 4,303
134 x 12 = 1,608
323 x 20 = 6,460
441 x 12 = 5,292
312 x 22 = 6,864
104 x 21 = 2,184
143 x 20 = 2,860
312 x 13 = 4,056
441 x 21 = 9,261
312 x 32 = 9,984

3 digits x 2 digits without regrouping **47**

Tasty Treats

Read.
Solve each problem on another sheet of paper.
Write your answer in the blank.

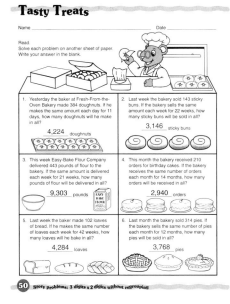

1. Yesterday the baker at Fresh-From-the-Oven Bakery made 384 doughnuts. If he makes the same amount each day for 11 days, how many doughnuts will he make in all?
4,224 doughnuts

2. Last week the bakery sold 143 sticky buns. If the bakery sells the same amount each week for 22 weeks, how many sticky buns will be sold in all?
3,146 sticky buns

3. This week Easy-Bake Flour Company delivered 443 pounds of flour to the bakery. If the same amount is delivered each week for 21 weeks, how many pounds of flour will be delivered in all?
9,303 pounds

4. This month the bakery received 210 orders for birthday cakes. If the bakery receives the same number of orders each month for 14 months, how many orders will be received in all?
2,940 orders

5. Last week the baker made 102 loaves of bread. If he makes the same number of loaves each week for 42 weeks, how many loaves will he bake in all?
4,284 loaves

6. Last month the bakery sold 314 pies. If the bakery sells the same number of pies each month for 12 months, how many pies will be sold in all?
3,768 pies

Story problems: 3 digits x 2 digits without regrouping **50**

Room for One More?

Multiply.
Show your work on another sheet of paper.
Color by the code.

Color Code
100–300 = orange
301–600 = green
601–900 = red
901–1,000 = blue

34 x 20 = 680
23 x 23 = 529
24 x 12 = 288
31 x 13 = 403
44 x 21 = 924
17 x 10 = 170
87 x 11 = 957
33 x 22 = 726
19 x 11 = 209
13 x 11 = 143
22 x 14 = 308
41 x 21 = 861

2 digits x 2 digits without regrouping **45**

And the Winner Is...

Multiply.
Show your work on another sheet of paper.
Color to show the path to the winner's ribbon.

Big Race Today!

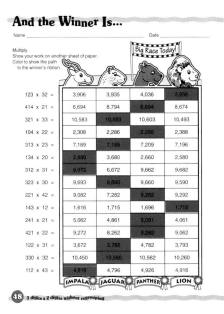

123 x 32 =	3,906	3,935	4,036	3,936
414 x 21 =	6,694	8,794	8,694	8,674
321 x 33 =	10,583	10,593	10,603	10,493
104 x 22 =	2,308	2,286	2,288	2,388
313 x 23 =	7,189	7,199	7,209	7,196
134 x 20 =	2,680	3,680	2,660	2,580
312 x 31 =	9,672	6,672	9,662	9,682
323 x 30 =	9,693	9,690	9,660	9,590
221 x 42 =	9,082	7,282	9,282	9,292
143 x 12 =	1,616	1,715	1,696	1,718
241 x 21 =	5,062	4,861	5,061	4,061
421 x 22 =	9,272	8,262	9,262	9,062
122 x 31 =	3,672	3,782	4,782	3,793
330 x 32 =	10,450	10,560	10,562	10,260
112 x 43 =	4,816	4,796	4,836	4,916

IMPALA JAGUAR PANTHER LION

3 digits x 2 digits without regrouping **48**

Floating on Cloud Nine

Multiply.
Show your work.
To solve the riddle, write the letter of each answer in its matching numbered blank below.

Cloud Nine

1,434 x 22 = 31,548	4,113 x 12 = 49,356	6,894 x 11 = 75,834
S	Y	T

2,304 x 21 = 48,384	3,012 x 32 = 96,384	1,301 x 33 = 42,933
E	T	U

1,220 x 43 = 52,460	2,021 x 14 = 28,294
B	E

Who put Billy Bob on Cloud Nine?

B   E   T   T   Y   _   S   U   E
52,460 48,384 75,834 96,384 49,356   31,548 42,933 28,294

4 digits x 2 digits without regrouping **51**

Lighting the Way

Name _____ Date _____

Multiply.
Show your work.
Color the matching street lamp.

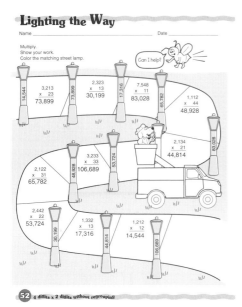

Can I help?

3,213
x 23
73,899

2,323
x 13
30,199

7,548
x 11
83,028

1,112
x 44
48,928

2,134
x 21
44,814

3,233
x 33
106,689

2,122
x 31
65,782

2,442
x 22
53,724

3,331
x 33
106,689

1,332
x 13
17,316

1,212
x 12
14,544

Lamp labels: 14,544 · 73,899 · 17,316 · 65,782 · 83,028 · 48,928 · 53,724 · 48,928 · 30,199 · 44,814 · 14,544

Fishin' for a Big One

Name _____ Date _____

Multiply.
Show your work.
Cross off each answer on the whale.
Some numbers will not be crossed off.

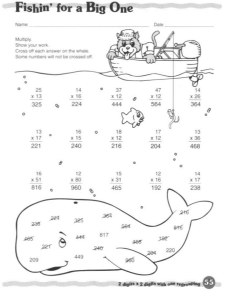

25
x 13
325

14
x 16
224

37
x 12
444

47
x 12
564

14
x 26
364

13
x 17
221

16
x 15
240

18
x 12
216

17
x 12
204

13
x 36
468

16
x 51
816

12
x 80
960

15
x 31
465

12
x 16
192

14
x 17
238

Whale numbers: 238 · 224 · 325 · 364 · 564 · 216 · 485 · 441 · 817 · 468 · 192 · 221 · 240 · 204 · 220 · 209 · 449 · 960

Mooseland Marvin

Name _____ Date _____

Read.
Solve each problem on another sheet of paper.
Write the answer in the blank.

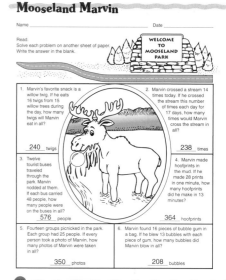

WELCOME TO MOOSELAND PARK

1. Marvin's favorite snack is a willow twig. If he eats 16 twigs from 15 willow trees during the day, how many twigs will Marvin eat in all?

__240__ twigs

2. Marvin crossed a stream 14 times today. If he crossed the stream this number of times each day for 17 days, how many times would Marvin cross the stream in all?

__238__ times

3. Twelve tourist buses traveled through the park. Marvin nodded at them. If each bus carried 48 people, how many people were on the buses in all?

__576__ people

4. Marvin made hoofprints in the mud. If he made 28 prints in one minute, how many hoofprints did he make in 13 minutes?

__364__ hoofprints

5. Fourteen groups picnicked in the park. Each group had 25 people. If every person took a photo of Marvin, how many photos of Marvin were taken in all?

__350__ photos

6. Marvin found 16 pieces of bubble gum in a bag. If he blew 13 bubbles with each piece of gum, how many bubbles did Marvin blow in all?

__208__ bubbles

Cornfield Conversation

Name _____ Date _____

Multiply.
Show your work on another sheet of paper.
To solve the riddle, match the letters on the husks to the numbered blanks below.
Some letters will not be used.

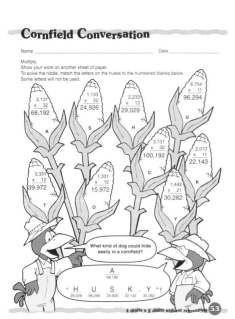

8,754
x 11
96,294

2,131
x 32
68,192

1,133
x 22
24,926

2,233
x 13
29,029

3,131
x 32
100,192

2,013
x 11
22,143

3,331
x 12
39,972

1,331
x 12
15,972

1,442
x 21
30,282

What kind of dog could hide easily in a cornfield?

__A__
68,192

" H   U   S   K   Y "!
29,029 96,294 24,926 22,143 30,282

Counting Sheep

Name _____ Date _____

Multiply.
Show your work on another sheet of paper.
Color if correct.

26
x 13
339

35
x 12
427

18
x 14
252

45
x 12
540

27
x 13
351

28
x 13
364

17
x 14
238

48
x 12
576

28
x 13
377

12
x 17
209

46
x 20
926

19
x 14
266

15
x 14
219

15
x 16
240

Sea of Stars

Name _____ Date _____

Multiply.
Show your work.
Color each starfish that has a matching answer.

218
x 14
3,052

291
x 21
6,111

108
x 17
1,836

121
x 38
4,598

145
x 12
1,740

181
x 41
7,421

109
x 71
7,739

113
x 37
4,181

262
x 13
3,406

141
x 27
3,807

140
x 72
10,080

371
x 12
4,452

Star numbers: 8,938 · 6,111 · 1,836 · 4,181 · 1,740 · 3,807 · 8,080 · 4,598 · 4,452 · 3,406 · 3,052 · 10,080 · 1,121 · 4,498 · 7,739

Meet the Rock Hounds!

Name _____ Date _____

Read.
Solve each problem on another sheet of paper.
Write the answer in the blank.

1. The Rock Hounds have 3,102 tickets to sell for a show. If the band sells this number of tickets for 32 shows, how many tickets will it sell in all?

__99,264__ tickets

2. After one show, 4,321 fans asked for autographed pictures. If the band gets this number of requests at 11 shows, how many requests will it get in all?

__47,531__ requests

3. A radio station got 1,043 requests in one week for the band's newest song. At this rate, how many requests for that song will the station get in 21 weeks?

__21,903__ requests

4. The group got 2,110 requests for Rock Hound T-shirts in one day. If the group gets this many requests for 31 days, how many requests will it get in all?

__65,410__ requests

5. The Rock Hounds traveled 1,122 miles last month. If the group travels that number of miles during each of 14 months, how many miles will it travel in all?

__15,708__ miles

6. Fans give stuffed animals to the band members. During the last tour, they got 2,303 stuffed animals. If the band gets this number on each of 13 different tours, how many stuffed animals will it have in all?

__29,939__ stuffed animals

Cool Cats

Name _____ Date _____

Multiply.
Show your work.
To answer the riddle, write the matching letters on the numbered lines below.

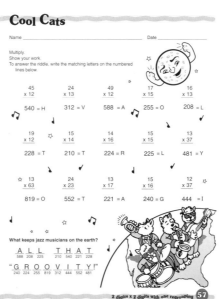

45
x 12
540 = H

24
x 13
312 = V

49
x 12
588 = A

17
x 15
255 = O

16
x 13
208 = L

19
x 12
228 = T

15
x 14
210 = T

14
x 16
224 = R

15
x 15
225 = L

13
x 37
481 = Y

13
x 63
819 = O

24
x 23
552 = T

13
x 17
221 = A

15
x 16
240 = G

12
x 37
444 = I

What keeps jazz musicians on the earth?

A   L   L   T   H   A   T
588 208 255   819 312 221 228

" G   R   O   O   V   I   T   Y "!
240 224 255 819 312 444 552 481

Heading Home!

Name _____ Date _____

Multiply.
Show your work on another sheet of paper.
Cross off each answer on the rocket.
Some numbers will not be crossed off.

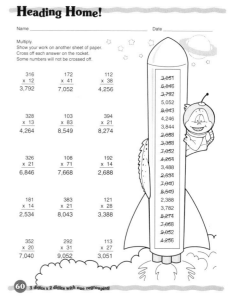

316
x 12
3,792

172
x 41
7,052

112
x 38
4,256

328
x 13
4,264

103
x 83
8,549

394
x 21
8,274

326
x 21
6,846

108
x 71
7,668

192
x 14
2,688

181
x 14
2,534

383
x 21
8,043

121
x 28
3,388

352
x 20
7,040

292
x 31
9,052

113
x 27
3,051

Rocket numbers: 3,051 · 6,846 · 3,792 · 5,052 · 8,043 · 4,246 · 3,844 · 2,688 · 3,388 · 7,052 · 4,264 · 2,534 · 7,040 · 8,549 · 2,388 · 8,274 · 7,668 · 4,256

T-Bone's Top Trick

Multiply.
Show your work on another sheet of paper.
Color to show the path to the best trick.

112 x 82 =	9,184	9,634	9,284	9,084
328 x 31 =	10,028	10,188	9,968	10,348
140 x 25 =	3,500	3,550	3,300	3,390
151 x 12 =	1,782	1,812	1,912	1,712
364 x 20 =	6,280	8,180	7,280	7,260
127 x 13 =	1,540	1,731	1,642	1,651
242 x 24 =	5,728	5,708	5,808	6,258
231 x 14 =	3,134	3,324	3,234	3,243
218 x 41 =	8,848	8,638	8,738	8,938
241 x 32 =	7,812	7,912	7,712	7,412
462 x 21 =	9,302	9,702	10,602	8,702
232 x 42 =	10,644	9,734	9,744	8,944

rolling over   chasing his tail   catching a ball   fetching a stick

---

Who Wins?

Multiply.
Show your work on another sheet of paper.
Color the boxes with the correct answers
to show the path to the winner.

4,112 x 42 =	172,714	172,704	172,604	162,704
1,813 x 12 =	21,755	21,735	21,756	21,736
3,152 x 21 =	66,293	66,203	66,193	66,192
2,231 x 24 =	52,544	53,594	53,544	53,545
3,613 x 21 =	75,874	75,873	75,883	76,073
1,116 x 15 =	16,740	16,741	16,761	17,740
1,604 x 12 =	19,246	19,248	19,268	19,276
1,801 x 14 =	25,254	25,315	25,214	25,215
4,021 x 13 =	52,263	52,274	52,273	52,264
2,421 x 23 =	55,583	55,683	55,673	55,674
2,013 x 24 =	38,312	48,312	48,212	48,412
4,201 x 42 =	176,442	176,443	176,462	176,423

Barney   Boomer   Bailey   Buster

Bull's-Eye!

Multiply.
Show your work.
Color by the code.

Code
odd = red
even = yellow

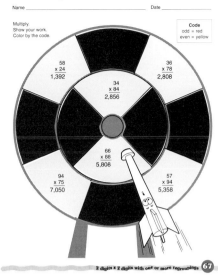

58 x 24 = 1,392
36 x 78 = 2,808
34 x 84 = 2,856
66 x 88 = 5,808
94 x 75 = 7,050
57 x 94 = 5,358

Zoo Zaniness

Read.
Solve each problem on another sheet of paper.
Write the answer in the blank.

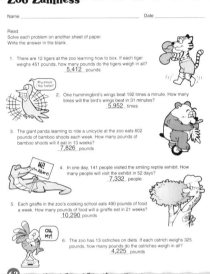

1. There are 12 tigers at the zoo learning how to box. If each tiger weighs 451 pounds, how many pounds do the tigers weigh in all?
   5,412 pounds

2. One hummingbird's wings beat 192 times a minute. How many times will the bird's wings beat in 31 minutes?
   5,952 times

3. The giant panda learning to ride a unicycle at the zoo eats 602 pounds of bamboo shoots each week. How many pounds of bamboo shoots will it eat in 13 weeks?
   7,826 pounds

4. In one day, 141 people visited the smiling reptile exhibit. How many people will visit the exhibit in 52 days?
   7,332 people

5. Each giraffe in the zoo's cooking school eats 490 pounds of food a week. How many pounds of food will a giraffe eat in 21 weeks?
   10,290 pounds

6. The zoo has 13 ostriches on diets. If each ostrich weighs 325 pounds, how many pounds do the ostriches weigh in all?
   4,225 pounds

Keeping Things Spiffy!

Multiply.
Show your work.
Color each letter that has a matching answer.

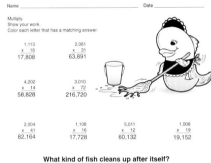

1,113 x 16 = 17,808
2,061 x 31 = 63,891
4,202 x 14 = 58,828
3,010 x 72 = 216,720
2,004 x 41 = 82,164
1,108 x 16 = 17,728
5,011 x 12 = 60,132
1,008 x 19 = 19,152

What kind of fish cleans up after itself?

A MERMAID

Nail It Down!

Multiply.
Show your work on another sheet of paper.
Write each letter in its matching blank below.

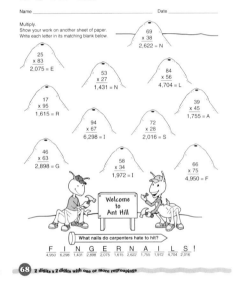

69 x 38 = 2,622 = N
25 x 83 = 2,075 = E
53 x 27 = 1,431 = N
84 x 56 = 4,704 = L
17 x 95 = 1,615 = R
39 x 45 = 1,755 = A
94 x 67 = 6,298 = I
72 x 28 = 2,016 = S
46 x 63 = 2,898 = G
58 x 34 = 1,972 = I
66 x 75 = 4,950 = F

Welcome to Ant Hill

What nails do carpenters hate to hit?

F I N G E R N A I L S !
4,950 6,298 1,431 2,898 1,615 2,622 1,755 1,972 4,704 2,016

Colossal Columns

Multiply.
Show your work.

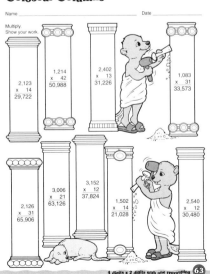

2,123 x 14 = 29,722
1,214 x 42 = 50,988
2,402 x 13 = 31,226
1,083 x 31 = 33,573
3,006 x 21 = 63,126
3,152 x 12 = 37,824
1,502 x 14 = 21,028
2,540 x 12 = 30,480
2,126 x 31 = 65,906

Taco Time!

Read.
Solve each problem on another sheet of paper.
Write the answer in the blank.

1. Paco has 12 big boxes of tacos. If each box holds 1,632 taco shells, how many shells does Paco have in all?
   19,584 shells

2. Paco has 15 different taco stands. If 1,102 tacos are sold at each stand, how many tacos will Paco sell in all?
   16,530 tacos

3. There are 14 large bags of shredded lettuce in Paco's refrigerator. If each bag contains 2,013 pieces of shredded lettuce, how many pieces does he have in all?
   28,182 pieces

4. Paco has 3,005 slices of cheese. If he shreds each slice into 13 pieces, how many cheese shreds will he have in all?
   39,065 shreds

5. There are 1,412 tomatoes being delivered to Paco's stand. If he cuts each tomato into 42 small cubes, how many cubes will he have in all?
   59,304 cubes

Right at Home!

Multiply.
Show your work on another sheet of paper.
Color if correct.

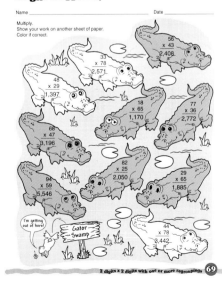

56 x 43 = 2,408
35 x 78 = 2,571
48 x 29 = 1,397
18 x 65 = 1,170
77 x 36 = 2,772
68 x 47 = 3,196
82 x 25 = 2,050
29 x 65 = 1,885
94 x 59 = 5,546
44 x 78 = 3,442

I'm getting out of here!
Gator Swamp

"Bone-a-fide" Doggie Treats

Read.
Solve each problem on another sheet of paper.
Write the answer in the blank.

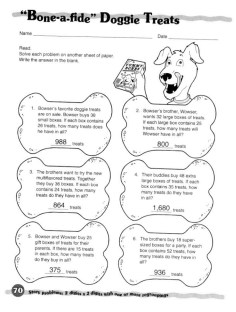

1. Bowser's favorite doggie treats are on sale. Bowser buys 38 small boxes. If each box contains 26 treats, how many treats does he have in all?

   988 treats

2. Bowser's brother, Wowser, wants 32 large boxes of treats. If each large box contains 25 treats, how many treats will Wowser have in all?

   800 treats

3. The brothers want to try the new multiflavored treats. Together they buy 36 boxes. If each box contains 24 treats, how many treats do they have in all?

   864 treats

4. Their buddies buy 48 extra large boxes of treats. If each box contains 35 treats, how many treats do they have in all?

   1,680 treats

5. Bowser and Wowser buy 25 gift boxes of treats for their parents. If there are 15 treats in each box, how many treats do they buy in all?

   375 treats

6. The brothers buy 18 super-sized boxes for a party. If each box contains 52 treats, how many treats do they have in all?

   936 treats

70 Story problems: 2 digits x 2 digits with one or more regroupings

---

Bank It!

Multiply.
Show your work on another sheet of paper.
Color the coins that have correct answers.

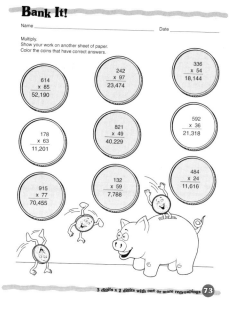

614 × 85 = 52,190

242 × 97 = 23,474

336 × 54 = 18,144

178 × 63 = 11,201

821 × 49 = 40,229

592 × 36 = 21,318

915 × 77 = 70,455

132 × 59 = 7,788

484 × 24 = 11,616

73 3 digits x 2 digits with one or more regroupings

Surrender?

Multiply.
Show your work on another sheet of paper.

Huh?

| 3,146 × 23 = 72,358 | 9,425 × 14 = 131,950 | 1,274 × 92 = 117,208 | 7,322 × 53 = 388,066 |

| 2,543 × 82 = 208,526 | 5,067 × 25 = 126,675 | 8,423 × 67 = 564,341 | 4,729 × 36 = 170,244 |

| 6,818 × 41 = 279,538 | 1,951 × 78 = 152,178 | 3,056 × 29 = 88,624 | 7,512 × 55 = 413,160 |

To find out what a white flag being waved in a car race means, color each space below that contains a correct answer.

208,525 73,358 151,178 8,014 216,675 31,950
413,160 88,624 564,341 170,244 208,526
117,218 126,675 152,178 14,35
3,546 279,528 279,538 218,526 152,179
11,431 512,871 413,150 8,624 88,635 170,234

76 4 digits x 2 digits with one or more regroupings

Let's Get Together!

Multiply.
Show your work.

We'll make a great pair!

| 287 × 33 = 9,471 | 394 × 52 = 20,488 | 456 × 39 = 17,784 |

| 165 × 84 = 13,860 | 506 × 88 = 44,528 | 637 × 92 = 58,604 |

| 714 × 63 = 44,982 | 820 × 46 = 37,720 | 959 × 73 = 70,007 |

71 3 digits x 2 digits with one or more regroupings

Getting the Scoop on Ice Cream

Read.
Solve each problem on another sheet of paper.
Write the answer in the blank.

1. Today, 516 cartons of ice cream arrived at Super Scoops Ice-Cream Shoppe. If each carton contains 23 scoops of ice cream, how many scoops can be served in all?

   11,868 scoops

2. Dippers Ice-Cream Company received a total of 842 orders for Choco-Berry ice cream. If the company gets that number of orders for 37 days, how many orders will it get in all?

   31,154 orders

3. If an ice-cream delivery truck can hold 329 cartons of ice cream, how many cartons can 65 trucks hold in all?

   21,385 cartons

4. Seventy-nine people scooped ice cream at Igloo Ice-Cream Store's grand opening. If each person made 284 scoops of ice cream, how many scoops were made in all?

   22,436 scoops

5. Igloo Ice-Cream Store gave away 188 plastic ice-cream scoopers each hour during its grand opening. If the grand opening lasted 24 hours, how many plastic scoopers were given away in all?

   4,512 plastic scoopers

6. Ida's Ice-Cream Shoppe gave away 782 free samples of ice cream today. If the shop gave away this number of samples each day for 48 days, how many samples would it give away in all?

   37,536 samples

74 Story problems: 3 digits x 2 digits with one or more regroupings

---

Goal!

Multiply.
Show your work on another sheet of paper.
Color if correct.
Connect the colored soccer balls to show the path to the goal.

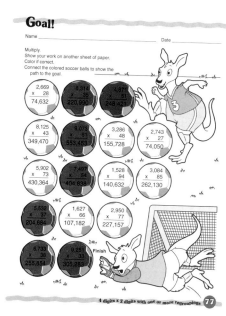

| 2,669 × 28 = 74,632 | 8,314 × 35 = 220,990 | 4,871 × 51 = 248,421 |

| 8,125 × 43 = 349,470 | 9,073 × 61 = 553,453 | 3,286 × 48 = 155,728 | 2,743 × 27 = 74,050 |

| 5,902 × 73 = 430,364 | 7,497 × 54 = 404,838 | 1,528 × 94 = 140,632 | 3,084 × 85 = 262,130 |

| 5,532 × 37 = 204,684 | 1,627 × 66 = 107,182 | 2,950 × 77 = 227,157 |

| 6,733 × 38 = 255,854 | 9,251 × 33 = 305,283 |

Finish

77 4 digits x 2 digits with one or more regroupings

Get a Strike!

Multiply.
Show your work.
To solve the riddle, write each letter in its matching blank.

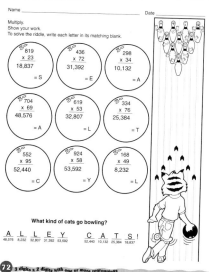

| 819 × 23 = 18,837 = S | 436 × 72 = 31,392 = E | 298 × 34 = 10,132 = A |

| 704 × 69 = 48,576 = A | 619 × 53 = 32,807 = L | 334 × 76 = 25,384 = T |

| 552 × 95 = 52,440 = C | 924 × 58 = 53,592 = Y | 168 × 49 = 8,232 = L |

What kind of cats go bowling?

A L L E Y   C A T S !
48,576 8,232 32,807 31,392 53,592   52,440 10,132 25,384 18,837

72 3 digits x 2 digits with one or more regroupings

Safe and Sound

Multiply.
Show your work.
Write each answer in the magic square. The sum of each row and column should be 500,000.

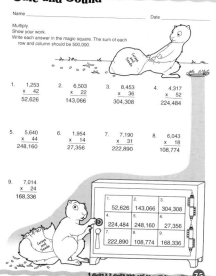

1. 1,253 × 42 = 52,626

2. 6,503 × 22 = 143,066

3. 8,453 × 36 = 304,308

4. 4,317 × 52 = 224,484

5. 5,640 × 44 = 248,160

6. 1,954 × 14 = 27,356

7. 7,190 × 31 = 222,890

8. 6,043 × 18 = 108,774

9. 7,014 × 24 = 168,336

1. 52,626	2. 143,066	3. 304,308
4. 224,484	5. 248,160	6. 27,356
7. 222,890	8. 108,774	9. 168,336

75 4 digits x 2 digits with one or more regroupings

Ants on Parade

Read.
Solve each problem on another sheet of paper.
Write the answer in the blank.

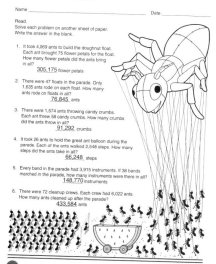

1. It took 4,069 ants to build the doughnut float. Each ant brought 75 flower petals for the float. How many flower petals did the ants bring in all?

   305,175 flower petals

2. There were 47 floats in the parade. Only 1,635 ants rode on each float. How many ants rode on floats in all?

   76,845 ants

3. There were 1,574 ants throwing candy crumbs. Each ant threw 58 candy crumbs. How many crumbs did the ants throw in all?

   91,292 crumbs

4. It took 26 ants to hold the great ant balloon during the parade. Each of the ants walked 2,548 steps. How many steps did the ants take in all?

   66,248 steps

5. Every band in the parade had 3,915 instruments. If 38 bands marched in the parade, how many instruments were there in all?

   148,770 instruments

6. There were 72 cleanup crews. Each crew had 6,022 ants. How many ants cleaned up after the parade?

   433,584 ants

78 Story problems: 4 digits x 2 digits with one or more regroupings

What's Cooking?

Name _____ Date _____

Multiply.
Cross off each answer on the spoon.
Some numbers will not be crossed off.

324 x 192 62,208	898 x 207 185,886	462 x 116 53,592
528 x 633 334,224	275 x 319 87,725	924 x 786 726,264
653 x 218 142,354	885 x 671 593,835	759 x 596 452,364
		463 x 781 361,603

Spoon numbers:
728,264
185,836
593,835
334,224
87,705
142,354
185,886
53,592
87,725
452,364
361,603
62,208
142,334

3 digits x 3 digits with one or more regroupings **79**

A Really Wild School

Name _____ Date _____

Multiply.
Show your work on another sheet of paper.
Write each answer in the blank.

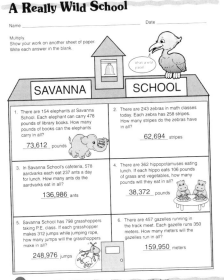

SAVANNA SCHOOL

1. There are 154 elephants at Savanna School. Each elephant can carry 478 pounds of library books. How many pounds of books can the elephants carry in all?
   73,612 pounds

2. There are 243 zebras in math classes today. Each zebra has 258 stripes. How many stripes do the zebras have in all?
   62,694 stripes

3. In Savanna School's cafeteria, 578 aardvarks each eat 237 ants a day for lunch. How many ants do the aardvarks eat in all?
   136,986 ants

4. There are 362 hippopotamuses eating lunch. If each hippo eats 106 pounds of grass and vegetables, how many pounds will they eat in all?
   38,372 pounds

5. Savanna School has 798 grasshoppers taking P.E. class. If each grasshopper makes 312 jumps while jumping rope, how many jumps will the grasshoppers make in all?
   248,976 jumps

6. There are 457 gazelles running in the track meet. Each gazelle runs 350 meters. How many meters will the gazelles run in all?
   159,950 meters

82 Story problems: 3 digits x 3 digits with one or more regroupings

---

Open Wide!

Name _____ Date _____

Multiply.
Show your work.
To solve the riddle, match the letters to the numbered lines below.

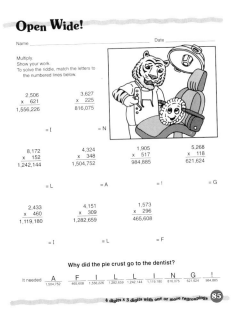

2,506 x 621 1,556,226	3,627 x 225 816,075		
= I	= N		
8,172 x 152 1,242,144	4,324 x 348 1,504,752	1,905 x 517 984,885	5,268 x 118 621,624
= L	= A	= !	= G
2,433 x 460 1,119,180	4,151 x 309 1,282,659	1,573 x 296 465,608	
= I	= L	= F	

Why did the pie crust go to the dentist?

It needed A_{1,504,752} F_{465,608} I_{1,556,226} L_{1,282,659} L_{1,242,144} I_{1,119,180} N_{816,075} G_{621,624} !_{984,885}

4 digits x 3 digits with one or more regroupings **85**

Whale Watch

Name _____ Date _____

Multiply.
Show your work on another sheet of paper.
Color to show the path to the whale.

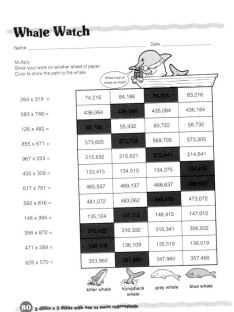

What kind of whale is that?

264 x 319 =	74,216	84,186	84,216	83,216
583 x 748 =	436,064	436,084	435,084	436,184
126 x 482 =	60,732	55,932	60,722	58,732
855 x 671 =	573,605	573,705	569,705	573,305
967 x 223 =	215,632	215,621	215,641	214,641
435 x 309 =	133,415	134,515	134,375	134,415
617 x 761 =	465,537	469,137	468,637	469,537
592 x 816 =	481,072	483,062	483,072	473,072
148 x 994 =	135,124	147,112	146,412	147,012
356 x 872 =	310,432	310,332	310,341	306,932
471 x 289 =	136,119	136,109	135,519	136,019
628 x 570 =	353,960	357,960	347,960	357,460

killer whale   humpback whale   gray whale   blue whale

80 3 digits x 3 digits with one or more regroupings

Baby's First Picture

Name _____ Date _____

Multiply.
Show your work.

Smile!

1,483 x 715 1,060,345	2,714 x 326 884,764	
5,062 x 239 1,209,818	3,918 x 454 1,778,772	1,635 x 182 297,570
6,401 x 395 2,528,395	2,341 x 513 1,200,933	

4 digits x 3 digits with one or more regroupings **83**

Opal's Orchard

Name _____ Date _____

Read.
Solve each problem on another sheet of paper.
Write the answer in the blank.

1. There are 1,425 apple trees in Opal's orchard. Each tree has 215 apples. How many apples are there in all? **306,375** apples

2. After sorting out the wormy apples, Opal has 2,067 bushels of apples. There are 144 apples in each bushel. How many wormless apples does Opal have? **297,648** wormless apples

3. Opal has 2,909 pounds of wormy apples. There are 113 worms in each pound. How many worms are there in all? **328,717** worms

4. Opal uses ladybugs for pest control. She bought 368 cartons of ladybugs. Each carton has 1,538 ladybugs inside. How many ladybugs are there in all? **565,984** ladybugs

5. If Opal's orchard needs 7,515 gallons of water a day, how many gallons will it need for 189 days? **1,420,335** gallons of water

6. Opal plants 1,594 rows of apple seeds. She puts 572 seeds in each row. How many apple seeds does she plant in all? **911,768** apple seeds

86 Story problems: 4 digits x 3 digits with one or more regroupings

---

Monkey Business

Name _____ Date _____

Multiply.
Show your work on another sheet of paper.
To solve the riddle, match the letters to the numbered blanks below.

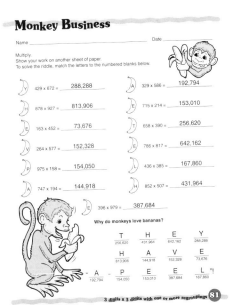

429 x 672 =	**288,288**		329 x 586 =	**192,794**
878 x 927 =	**813,906**		715 x 214 =	**153,010**
163 x 452 =	**73,676**		658 x 390 =	**256,620**
264 x 577 =	**152,328**		786 x 817 =	**642,162**
975 x 158 =	**154,050**		436 x 385 =	**167,860**
747 x 194 =	**144,918**		852 x 507 =	**431,964**
		396 x 979 =	**387,684**	

Why do monkeys love bananas?

T_{256,620} H_{431,964} E_{73,676} Y_{288,288}
H_{813,906} A_{144,918} V_{152,328} E_{73,676}
A_{192,794} P_{154,050} E_{153,010} E_{387,684} L_{167,860} "!

3 digits x 3 digits with one or more regroupings **81**

Bunches of Butterflies

Name _____ Date _____

Multiply.
Show your work on another sheet of paper.
Color by the code.

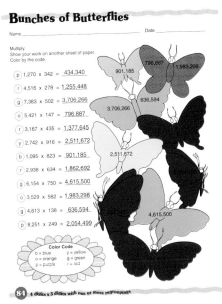

p 1,270 x 342 = **434,340**
r 4,516 x 278 = **1,255,448**
g 7,383 x 502 = **3,706,266**
o 5,421 x 147 = **796,887**
r 3,167 x 435 = **1,377,645**
y 2,742 x 916 = **2,511,672**
b 1,095 x 823 = **901,185**
r 2,938 x 634 = **1,862,692**
g 6,154 x 750 = **4,615,500**
o 3,529 x 562 = **1,983,298**
g 4,613 x 138 = **636,594**
p 8,251 x 249 = **2,054,499**

Color Code
b = blue   y = yellow
o = orange   g = green
p = purple   r = red

84 4 digits x 3 digits with one or more regroupings

Outer Space or Bust!

Name _____ Date _____

Color each star that shows the commutative property.

Finish

93 x 12 = 1,116
18 x 62 = 1,116

28 x 11 = 308
11 x 28 = 308

78 x 6 = 450
6 x 75 = 450

610 x 7 = 4,270
7 x 610 = 4,270

23 x 41 = 943
40 x 23 = 920

8 x 7 = 56
4 x 14 = 56

53 x 5 = 165
5 x 33 = 165

120 x 50 = 6,000
600 x 10 = 6,000

9 x 8 = 72
8 x 19 = 72

16 x 24 = 384
32 x 12 = 384

47 x 12 = 564
12 x 47 = 564

17 x 21 = 357
21 x 17 = 357

25 x 103 = 2,575
103 x 25 = 2,575

50 x 4 = 200
4 x 25 = 200

56 x 14 = 784
16 x 49 = 784

45 x 3 = 135
46 x 3 = 138

18 x 3 = 54
9 x 6 = 54

90 x 2 = 180
3 x 60 = 180

13 x 3 = 39
3 x 13 = 39

6 x 6 = 48
6 x 7 = 42

Start

7 x 25 = 175
25 x 7 = 175

9 x 7 = 63
7 x 9 = 63

Commutative Property **89**

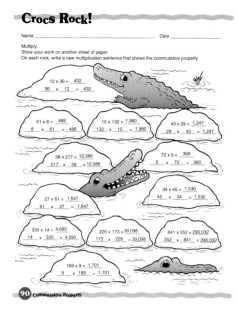

Crocs Rock!

Name _____ Date _____

Multiply.
Show your work on another sheet of paper.
On each rock, write a new multiplication sentence that shows the commutative property.

12 x 36 = 432
36 x 12 = 432

61 x 8 = 488
8 x 61 = 488

15 x 132 = 1,980
132 x 15 = 1,980

34 x 29 = 1,247
29 x 43 = 1,247

58 x 217 = 12,586
217 x 58 = 12,586

72 x 5 = 360
5 x 72 = 360

27 x 61 = 1,647
61 x 27 = 1,647

34 x 45 = 1,530
45 x 34 = 1,530

335 x 14 = 4,690
14 x 335 = 4,690

226 x 173 = 39,098
173 x 226 = 39,098

841 x 352 = 296,032
352 x 841 = 296,032

189 x 9 = 1,701
9 x 189 = 1,701

90 Commutative Property

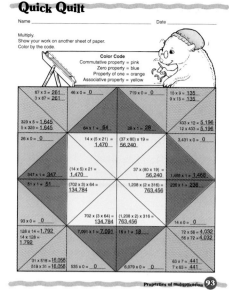

Quick Quilt

Name _____ Date _____

Multiply.
Show your work on another sheet of paper.
Color by the code.

Color Code
Commutative property = pink
Zero property = blue
Property of one = orange
Associative property = yellow

87 x 3 = 261
3 x 87 = 261

46 x 0 = 0

719 x 0 = 0

15 x 9 = 135
9 x 15 = 135

329 x 5 = 1,645
5 x 329 = 1,645

64 x 1 = 64

28 x 1 = 28

433 x 12 = 5,196
12 x 433 = 5,196

26 x 0 = 0

14 x (5 x 21) = 1,470

(37 x 80) x 19 = 56,240

847 x 1 = 347

(14 x 5) x 21 = 1,470

37 x (80 x 19) = 56,240

51 x 1 = 51

(702 x 3) x 64 = 134,784

1,208 x (2 x 316) = 763,456

238 x 1 = 236

93 x 0 = 0

702 x (3 x 64) = 134,784

(1,208 x 2) x 316 = 763,456

14 x 0 = 0

128 x 14 = 1,792
14 x 128 = 1,792

7,091 x 1 = 7,091

18 x 1 = 18

72 x 56 = 4,032
56 x 72 = 4,032

31 x 518 = 16,058
518 x 31 = 16,058

535 x 0 = 0

6,079 x 0 = 0

63 x 7 = 441
7 x 63 = 441

Properties of multiplication **93**

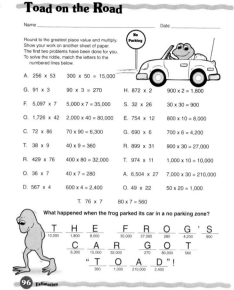

Toad on the Road

Name _____ Date _____

Round to the greatest place value and multiply.
Show your work on another sheet of paper.
The first two problems have been done for you.
To solve the riddle, match the letters to the numbered lines below.

A. 256 x 53   300 x 50 = 15,000
G. 91 x 3   90 x 3 = 270
H. 872 x 2   900 x 2 = 1,800
F. 5,097 x 7   5,000 x 7 = 35,000
S. 32 x 26   30 x 30 = 900
O. 1,726 x 42   2,000 x 40 = 80,000
E. 754 x 12   800 x 10 = 8,000
C. 72 x 86   70 x 90 = 6,300
G. 690 x 6   700 x 6 = 4,200
T. 38 x 9   40 x 9 = 360
R. 899 x 31   900 x 30 = 27,000
R. 429 x 76   400 x 80 = 32,000
T. 974 x 11   1,000 x 10 = 10,000
O. 36 x 7   40 x 7 = 280
A. 6,504 x 27   7,000 x 30 = 210,000
D. 567 x 4   600 x 4 = 2,400
O. 49 x 22   50 x 20 = 1,000
T. 76 x 7   80 x 7 = 560

What happened when the frog parked its car in a no parking zone?

T H E   F R O G ' S
10,000 1,800   35,000 270 280 4,200 900

C A R   G O T
6,300 15,000 32,000 70 80,000 560

" T O A D "!
360 1,000 210,000 2,400

96 Estimation

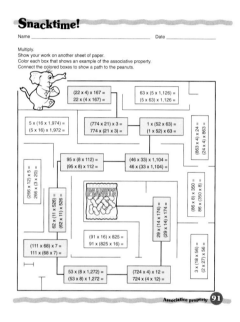

Snacktime!

Name _____ Date _____

Multiply.
Show your work on another sheet of paper.
Color each box that shows an example of the associative property.
Connect the colored boxes to show a path to the peanuts.

(22 x 4) x 167 =
22 x (4 x 167) =

63 x (5 x 1,126) =
(5 x 63) x 1,126 =

5 x (16 x 1,974) =
(5 x 16) x 1,972 =

(774 x 21) x 3 =
774 x (21 x 3) =

1 x (52 x 63) =
(1 x 52) x 63 =

(863 x 4) x 24 =
(24 x 4) x 863 =

95 x (8 x 112) =
(95 x 8) x 112 =

(46 x 33) x 1,104 =
46 x (33 x 1,104) =

(266 x 12) x 5 =
266 x (3 x 20) =

62 x (11 x 526) =
(62 x 11) x 526 =

PEANUTS

(86 x 81) x 350 =
86 x (350 x 8) =

(111 x 68) x 7 =
111 x (68 x 7) =

(91 x 16) x 825 =
91 x (825 x 16) =

29 x (14 x 174) =
(29 x 14) x 174 =

3 x (18 x 56) =
(2 x 27) x 56 =

53 x (8 x 1,272) =
(53 x 8) x 1,272 =

(724 x 4) x 12 =
724 x (4 x 12) =

Associative property **91**

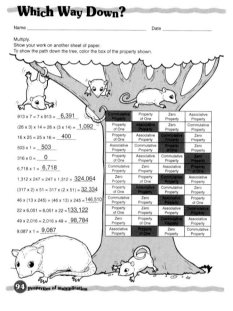

Which Way Down?

Name _____ Date _____

Multiply.
Show your work on another sheet of paper.
To show the path down the tree, color the box of the property shown.

913 x 7 = 7 x 913 = 6,391

(26 x 3) x 14 = 26 x (3 x 14) = 1,092

16 x 25 = 25 x 16 = 400

503 x 1 = 503

316 x 0 = 0

6,718 x 1 = 6,718

1,312 x 247 = 247 x 1,312 = 324,064

(317 x 2) x 51 = 317 x (2 x 51) = 32,334

46 x (13 x 245) = (46 x 13) x 245 = 146,510

22 x 6,051 = 6,051 x 22 = 133,122

49 x 2,016 = 2,016 x 49 = 98,784

9,087 x 1 = 9,087

Commutative	Property of One	Zero Property	Associative Property
Property of One	Associative Property	Associative Property	Commutative Property
Property of One	Associative Property	Commutative Property	Zero Property
Associative Property	Zero Property	Associative Property	Property of One
Zero Property	Commutative Property	Associative Property	Zero Property
Commutative Property	Associative Property	Associative Property	Property of One
Zero Property	Property of One	Commutative Property	Associative Property
Commutative Property	Zero Property	Associative Property	Property of One
Property of One	Zero Property	Associative Property	Commutative Property
Zero Property	Property of One	Commutative Property	Associative Property
Associative Property	Property of One	Zero Property	Commutative Property

94 Properties of multiplication

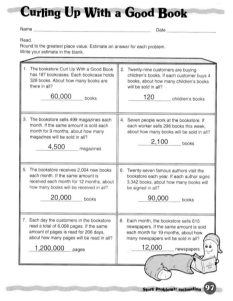

Curling Up With a Good Book

Name _____ Date _____

Read.
Round to the greatest place value. Estimate an answer for each problem.
Write your estimate in the blank.

1. The bookstore Curl Up With a Good Book has 187 bookcases. Each bookcase holds 328 books. About how many books are there in all?
60,000 books

2. Twenty-nine customers are buying children's books. If each customer buys 4 books, about how many children's books are sold in all?
120 children's books

3. The bookstore sells 499 magazines each month. If the same amount is sold each month for 9 months, about how many magazines will be sold in all?
4,500 magazines

4. Seven people work at the bookstore. If each worker sells 296 books this week, about how many books will be sold in all?
2,100 books

5. The bookstore receives 2,004 new books each month. If the same amount is received each month for 12 months, about how many books will be received in all?
20,000 books

6. Twenty-seven famous authors visit the bookstore each year. If each author signs 3,342 books, about how many books will be signed in all?
90,000 books

7. Each day the customers in the bookstore read a total of 6,008 pages. If the same amount of pages is read for 206 days, about how many pages will be read in all?
1,200,000 pages

8. Each month, the bookstore sells 615 newspapers. If the same amount is sold each month for 19 months, about how many newspapers will be sold in all?
12,000 newspapers

Story Problems: estimation **97**

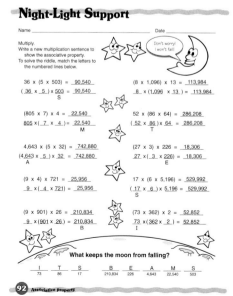

Night-Light Support

Name _____ Date _____

Multiply.
Write a new multiplication sentence to show the associative property.
To solve the riddle, match the letters to the numbered lines below.

Don't worry!
I won't fall!

36 x (5 x 503) = 90,540
(36 x 5) x 503 = 90,540
S

(8 x 1,096) x 13 = 113,984
8 x (1,096 x 13) = 113,984
T

(805 x 7) x 4 = 22,540
805 x (7 x 4) = 22,540
M

52 x (86 x 64) = 286,208
(52 x 86) x 64 = 286,208
T

4,643 x (5 x 32) = 742,880
(4,643 x 5) x 32 = 742,880
A

(27 x 3) x 226 = 18,306
27 x (3 x 226) = 18,306
E

(9 x 4) x 721 = 25,956
9 x (4 x 721) = 25,956

17 x (6 x 5,196) = 529,992
(17 x 6) x 5,196 = 529,992
S

(9 x 901) x 26 = 210,834
9 x (901 x 26) = 210,834
B

(73 x 362) x 2 = 52,852
73 x (362 x 2) = 52,852
I

What keeps the moon from falling?

____ ____ ____ ____ ____ ____ ____
73   86   17   210,834   4,643   22,540   503
I   T   S   B   E   A   M   S

92 Associative Property

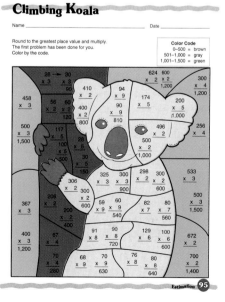

Climbing Koala

Name _____ Date _____

Round to the greatest place value and multiply.
The first problem has been done for you.
Color by the code.

Color Code
0–500 = brown
501–1,000 = gray
1,001–1,500 = green

26 → 30
x 3   x 3
      90

624 600
x 2   x 2
1,200

300
x 4
1,200

410
x 2

94
x 9

174
x 5

200
x 5
1,000

458
x 2

56 60
x 2 x 2
400
x 2
800

90
x 2
810

500
x 3
1,500

117
x 2

100
x 5
500

496
x 2

256
x 4

325 300
x 3   x 3
600

298
x 2
600

533
x 3

306
x 3
300

500
x 3
1,500

367
x 3

206
x 2
400

59 60
x 9 x 9
540

82
x 7

400
x 3
1,200

67
x 2

91 90
x 8 x 8

129
x 6

100
x 6

672
x 2

70
x 2
280

68 70
x 9 x 9
630

76 80
x 8 x 8
640

700
x 2
1,400

Estimation **95**

Afternoon Snooze Tune

Name _____ Date _____

Color the notes that are multiples of 10.

801
408
906
56
505
201

98 Multiples of 10

135

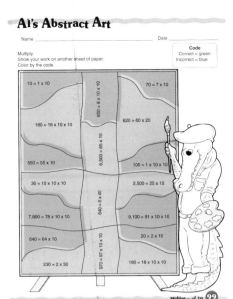

Al's Abstract Art

Name _____ Date _____

Multiply.
Show your work on another sheet of paper.
Color by the code.

Code
Correct = green
Incorrect = blue

10 = 1 x 10

600 = 8 x 10 x 10

70 = 7 x 10

180 = 18 x 10 x 10

620 = 60 x 20

6,500 = 65 x 10

550 = 55 x 10

100 = 1 x 10 x 10

30 = 10 x 10 x 10

2,500 = 25 x 10

7,800 = 78 x 10 x 10

640 = 6 x 40

9,100 = 91 x 10 x 10

640 = 64 x 10

20 = 2 x 10

230 = 2 x 30

970 = 97 x 10 x 10

180 = 18 x 10 x 10

Multiples of 10 99

Sandwich and Bag Matchup

Name _____ Date _____

Multiply.
Show your work on another sheet of paper.
Write the answer in the blank.
Color by the code.

Code
300 = red   5,400 = brown
900 = yellow   6,000 = orange
1,300 = purple   7,600 = blue
4,000 = green   85,000 = pink
790,000 = gray

79 x 10⁴ =
790,000

79 x 10 x 10 x 10 x 10 =
790,000

4 x 10 x 10 x 10 =
4,000

54 x 10 x 10 =
5,400

54 x 10² =
5,400

9 x 10 x 10 =
900

76 x 10² =
7,600

85 x 10² =
85,000

76 x 10 x 10 =
7,600

6 x 10³ =
6,000

85 x 10 x 10 x 10 =
85,000

9 x 10² =
900

4 x 10³ =
4,000

6 x 10 x 10 x 10 =
6,000

100 Multiples of 10

Page 105
Checkup 1
Test A
A. 96, 88, 24, 84, 66
B. 28, 84, 36, 80, 55
C. 88, 99, 42, 68, 33
D. 77, 60, 60, 48, 69

Test B
A. 46, 90, 66, 86, 88
B. 66, 48, 93, 80, 44
C. 90, 64, 99, 82, 63
D. 26, 62, 39, 28, 44

Page 107
Checkup 2
Test A
A. 948, 568, 750, 474
B. 926, 657, 984, 814
C. 306, 924, 378, 912

Test B
A. 810, 608, 722, 729
B. 681, 964, 786, 464
C. 748, 832, 576, 838

Page 109
Checkup 3
Test A
A. 16,492; 33,060; 59,297
B. 28,359; 61,456; 3,632
C. 21,372; 18,864; 16,581
D. 39,070; 25,448; 39,932

Test B
A. 19,740; 10,656; 16,914
B. 40,584; 14,052; 39,234
C. 36,792; 66,123; 19,460
D. 16,935; 41,490; 36,252

Page 111
Checkup 4
Test A
A. 504, 714, 276
B. 385, 286, 483
C. 946, 198, 759

Test B
A. 682, 288, 319
B. 396, 903, 506
C. 737, 294, 516

Page 113
Checkup 5
Test A
A. 8,432; 8,520; 5,580; 9,513
B. 2,982; 3,419; 6,642; 5,892
C. 8,274; 5,760; 3,794; 8,757

Test B
A. 3,048; 10,912; 9,891; 4,720
B. 3,653; 8,300; 6,810; 1,512
C. 1,968; 9,579; 8,897; 3,864

Page 115
Checkup 6
Test A
A. 82,460; 408,022; 208,307
B. 226,137; 142,128; 180,180
C. 279,538; 88,624; 248,421

Test B
A. 102,080; 145,002; 359,632
B. 232,826; 131,950; 158,002
C. 157,728; 349,375; 262,140

Page 117
Checkup 7
Test A
A. 180,411; 86,500; 424,545
B. 228,744; 556,156; 52,548
C. 307,440; 94,285; 215,929

Test B
A. 280,224; 123,453; 615,730
B. 664,884; 391,326; 115,166
C. 242,432; 326,610; 83,000

Page 119
Checkup 8
Test A
A. 497,029; 884,764; 330,315
B. 3,316,555; 1,200,933; 1,347,478

Test B
A. 1,377,772; 1,209,818; 2,023,623
B. 652,464; 434,340; 3,585,716